Defusing the Sexuality Debate

Defusing the Sexuality Debate

Anglican Evangelicals in Conflict

Mark Vasey-Saunders

scm press

© Mark Vasey-Saunders 2023

Published in 2023 by SCM Press
Editorial office
3rd Floor, Invicta House,
108–114 Golden Lane,
London EC1Y 0TG, UK

www.scmpress.co.uk

SCM Press is an imprint of Hymns Ancient & Modern Ltd
(a registered charity)

Hymns Ancient & Modern® is a registered trademark of
Hymns Ancient & Modern Ltd
13A Hellesdon Park Road, Norwich,
Norfolk NR6 5DR, UK

All rights reserved. No part of this publication may be reproduced,
stored in a retrieval system, or transmitted,
in any form or by any means, electronic, mechanical,
photocopying or otherwise, without the prior permission of
the publisher, SCM Press.

Mark Vasey-Saunders has asserted his right under the
Copyright, Designs and Patents Act 1988 to be identified
as the Author of this Work

British Library Cataloguing in Publication data

A catalogue record for this book is available
from the British Library

978-0-334-06354-4

Typeset by Regent Typesetting
Printed and bound in Great Britain by
CPI Group (UK) Ltd

Contents

Introduction vii

1 Evangelicals talking about sexuality:
  The creation of the consensus position 1
2 Evangelicals talking about scripture 38
3 Evangelicals talking to evangelicals 78
4 Evangelicals talking about modernity:
  The question behind the question 115
5 Advice to a divided church 162

Appendix: A timeline for evangelicalism and sexuality
in the twentieth and twenty-first centuries 178

Further reading 185
Index of Names and Subjects 193

Introduction

The sexuality debate has become a battlefield. Armies of progressives and conservatives shell each other constantly from entrenched positions. Behind the lines of each side they tell each other stories of the atrocities the other side has committed and the glorious victory they seek to achieve in order to keep up the morale of the exhausted troops on the front line. And in between the two is the minefield of the debate itself – an inhospitable middle ground, where every contour has been carefully mapped out, every approach carefully plotted and turned into a deathtrap. To go over the top into the debate itself is to constantly risk treading on a mine through a careless turn of phrase or unconsidered scriptural reference. Authenticity is called for, but rarely rewarded. Expressing your convictions honestly can open you to attack from the other side. Expressing your doubts honestly can lead to an over-zealous sniper from your own side taking a shot at you. So debate becomes guarded, performative, and settles into the predictable contours of stalemate. A few well-known figures periodically emerge from each side to rehearse well-known views. The intent is more to reassure their own side that their truth is being spoken than it is to enter into genuine dialogue with anyone else. At times the statements are so disconnected from each other it is hard to be sure the two sides are even fighting the same battle. Most prefer to stay huddled in the security of their own side, keeping their certainties or their doubts to themselves, not risking poking a head above the parapet. The war grinds on. Both sides fear they are constantly on the edge of defeat and cannot risk giving the slightest ground. Both fear that no victory will be sustainable that falls short of complete destruction of the enemy, meaning that the next phase of the war will be even worse than this trench warfare. Although both say they want nothing more than to stop fighting, they every day entrench themselves further.

Although a little fanciful, I don't think the above is too far off the mark in naming the experience of the church's debate over sexuality. It has become destructive, and exerts a profoundly negative influence on all areas of church life, leaving casualties in its wake on both sides. Some have been persecuted. Some have been excluded from communities in which they were once welcomed and accepted. Some have been driven to despair and have left the church.

Given all of this, the question: 'Why write yet another book about sexuality?' is an obvious one. It might be helpful to first clarify what I am and am not seeking to do. I do not try to propose an answer to the debate itself. You will not find anywhere in these pages an argument for or against the Church of England's current settlement on sexuality. In many ways this book represents nothing more than exploring the ground on which the debate is occurring: a setting out of what might be involved in attempting to answer the question. The reason for this is that I have become convinced that at present we don't even agree on what the question is. As Oliver O'Donovan was to write perceptively of the sexuality debate over a decade ago: 'Everything is something other than what it is, everything is charged with borrowed significations ... A patient work of interpretation is needed. To try to handle the question peremptorily is to deny what it is we face.'[1] I seek to help defuse a debate that has become corrosive to the spiritual health of all those caught up in it, on both sides, by trying to unpick exactly what it is we are arguing about and why it has aroused such passionate intensity. I write as an evangelical Anglican, largely about evangelical Anglicans (though I hope much of what I write may be of benefit to those who are neither). For this reason much of my focus is on the rights and wrongs of evangelical Anglicans, though, because of the transatlantic nature of the sexuality debate, many of the evangelical writers with whom I engage

INTRODUCTION

are not Anglican. I do not doubt that a similar book could be written about the rights and wrongs of liberal understandings to the sexuality debate, but my concern is primarily to remove the plank in my own eye, before making any attempt to remove the speck in the eye of my brothers and sisters.

It is my conviction, then, that the sexuality debate has become destructive and intractable in part because it is rooted in some commonly held misconceptions and myths. I want to examine four areas, four ways in which we have allowed ourselves to misunderstand what is really at stake. The first two of these are misunderstandings about what I call the evangelical 'consensus position' – the understanding that the only permissible patterns of sexual life for gay or straight people are heterosexual marriage or abstinence, and the pattern of biblical interpretation underlying it. In Chapter 1 I explore where the consensus position as it is now stated comes from, and whether it is helpful or accurate to describe it as the tradition of the church. In Chapter 2 I trace some of the history of interpretation of the key biblical passages behind the consensus position and consider whether it is helpful or accurate to describe the interpretation offered as the clear sense of scripture. Having examined some of the history of the establishment of the consensus position, I then turn to examine the sexuality debate itself from two different perspectives. In Chapter 3 I explore the politicized nature of the debate, tracing the history of how it has become as destructive and intractable as I suggest above. Finally in Chapter 4 I explore the extent to which the sexuality debate is really a proxy war for a deeper conflict over the interpretation of modernity itself. In Chapter 5 I briefly reflect on this understanding of the debate and offer some suggestions to those of us caught up in it.

It will quickly become obvious that much of what I am attempting here will effectively act to undermine a key position defended by conservative evangelicals: the conviction that adherence to the consensus position represents a first order issue of faith, where disagreement represents unfaithfulness to the gospel. This is deliberate. I believe that this conviction is a major contributor to the current destructive state of debate, preventing genuine engagement with the issues ostensibly being discussed. For both sides the debate has become a nil sum game where they either win or they leave. This in itself would be a good pragmatic reason for challenging it, but I want to make the case that it is also fundamentally mistaken. None of the arguments commonly advanced as to why adherence to the consensus position should be considered a first order issue are compelling, in large part because they all represent a rush to judgement. At present I'm not convinced we even know what it is we are taking a stand to protect or to prevent. Similarly, I believe that the pattern of biblical interpretation on which the consensus position is based is far newer, and far less certain than much rhetoric would suggest, and that the passages on which it is based are considerably more complex to understand than is generally admitted.

None of this means that coming to an understanding of what scripture is saying to us is impossible, or that we do not have the obligation to sit under its judgement. It does not even mean that the consensus position itself is wrong – it may be the best attempt we can make at coming to the truth of scriptural witness. It simply means that discerning what the word of God is saying at this time is difficult, the more so when we may not properly understand the choice before us, and are actively seeking to invalidate the perspectives of those we do not agree with. As O'Donovan reminds us: 'The most mysterious question anyone has to face is not, what does Scripture mean? But, what does the situation I am facing mean?'[2] This is the task before us, and requires a careful act of discernment drawing on the wisdom of the whole church across our differences of opinion, but at present reaching across the divides to do this seems impossible. We find ourselves in the midst of an intractable, destructive and spiritually corrosive conflict, for which none of us are solely responsible, but in regard to which none of us are entirely innocent. Understanding where we are and how we got here may be a good first step.

It may help to define a few key terms I use throughout to avoid misunderstanding their meaning. I will use Church of England

INTRODUCTION

and Anglican fairly interchangeably. Although I am aware that the sexuality debate is wider than the Church of England (and at points I refer to transatlantic and Global South influences on and implications for the debate), the central focus of my discussion remains on the Church of England. For reasons that will become obvious in Chapter 1, I avoid the terms 'orthodox' and 'revisionist', which have become common in some circles, instead preferring the less loaded terms 'conservative' and 'progressive' as oriented vis-à-vis the current settlement of the Church of England in regard to sexuality. This is distinct from the 'party-political' labels of 'evangelical' and 'liberal', not least because although almost by definition all liberals tend to be progressive in regard to sexuality (though it is also true that there are more conservative liberals), there are both conservative and progressive evangelicals. Finally, I tend to use the terms 'modern' and 'modernity' to describe the current historical era. I explore understandings of modernity in Chapter 4, but for now it's helpful to note that I generally use this terminology in the sense employed by historians, who would apply the label to the period covering the last four to five hundred years. My decision to use the term 'modernity' in such a broad sense (and thus to avoid the use of terms like late- or post-modernity) is largely based on the conviction that, particularly in regard to sexuality, the socio-cultural changes of the last 50 years are best understood as natural developments of far more long-standing cultural shifts. This is an understanding shared by Carl Trueman, one of the more recent conservative evangelical writers on the subject: 'The sexual revolution did not cause the sexual revolution ... its causes lie much deeper, in the changes in what it meant to be an authentic, fulfilled human self. And those changes stretch back well before the Swinging Sixties.'[3]

Notes

1 O'Donovan, Oliver, 2009, *A Conversation Waiting to Begin*, London: SCM Press, p. 49.
2 O'Donovan, 2009, p. 59.
3 Trueman, Carl R., 2022, *The Rise and Triumph of the Modern Self*, Wheaton: Crossway, p. 23.

I

Evangelicals talking about sexuality: The creation of the consensus position

One thing that most people will accept unquestioningly in the increasingly contested war of words over sexuality is that conservatives represent the historical tradition of the church, which they have received unmodified and are seeking to defend against modern revisions. By contrast, progressives are understood as theological innovators, making a case for a new sexual ethic that departs from the received tradition of the church. Thus the conservative evangelical Glynn Harrison, in his *A Better Story* (2016) describes the impact of the sexual revolution of the Sixties:

> In the space of just a few decades the Christian moral vision, which had buttressed the ancient institutions of marriage and family for centuries, effectively collapsed ... those Christians who still cling to the old Christian morality understandably feel overwhelmed.[1]

Harrison therefore uses the term 'orthodox' to describe the conservative position. Even when acknowledging that conservatives are rightly repudiating an unbiblical sense of fear and shame (which he explicitly notes includes the repudiation of homophobia) in their discussion of sex and relationships, he does not characterize this as revising orthodoxy in the face of the sexual revolution.[2] Rather, he sees it as a simple restatement of the traditional orthodox teaching of the church.

Although it is clear that Harrison acknowledges modern evangelicals have rejected homophobia, and that this constituted a healthy change prompted by wider culture, this does not prevent him from unproblematically presenting conservatives as inheritors of an unchanged tradition. My argument in this chapter is that this sort of rhetorical minimizing of the significance of conservative revision of received tradition glosses over the significance of a profound shift in understanding. In fact, the creation of a non-homophobic version of Christian tradition that can be defended in the modern world represents a significant act of theological scholarship on the part of evangelicals in the second half of the twentieth century undertaken in order to distance themselves from both earlier tradition and modern liberal alternatives.

The evangelical consensus position

It is important to define the position defended by conservatives like Harrison before going any further in explaining how it came to exist in its current form. I will call this understanding of sexuality 'the evangelical consensus position', recognizing that it became widely accepted within evangelicalism from the Eighties until recently. A fairly non-controversial description of this understanding expressed in terms of church policy would be as follows:

- Homophobia is to be condemned, and all Christians are to be fully accepted as full members of the church, able to minister at all levels of the church regardless of sexual orientation (some evangelicals would argue that 'gay' is a cultural identity that they do not wish to adopt, and therefore avoid the language of 'gay' and 'straight', preferring the term 'same-sex attracted').
- Heterosexual marriage is the only context in which it is appropriate to have a sexual relationship. Same-sex sexual relationships therefore cannot be recognized as marriages

and it would be inappropriate to celebrate them in a church context or in any way suggest that they were equivalent to marriage. Sexual activity outside marriage is sinful whether gay or straight in nature, and should be set aside by faithful Christian disciples.

This basic approach of church policy towards questions of sexuality is based on a particular interpretation of scripture:

- The Genesis creation narratives set out an understanding of marriage that is based in the complementary created nature of men and women, resulting in a one-flesh union that is necessarily heterosexual. The centrality of this understanding of marriage is demonstrated by the reference made to this passage by Jesus, making it foundational for questions of sexual ethics. This interpretation can therefore be presented as the teaching of Christ.
- In the seven direct references to same-sex sexual relationships in the Bible it consistently presents a negative evaluation of them, and never makes any positive reference to them. These references occur in multiple different periods, different genres of writing, and consistently mark out the people of Israel and the early church as adopting a more conservative position on sexuality than surrounding cultures. It is therefore illegitimate to interpret scripture as permitting same-sex sexual relationships.

Both the interpretation of scripture and the church policy derived from it constitute the evangelical consensus position. It is at least compatible with and in some cases lies directly behind most current Church of England statements on sexuality, from General Synod's 'Higton motion' of 1987, to *Issues in Human Sexuality* in 1991, to the various Church of England submissions to government around the formulation of legislation for same-sex marriage. Significantly for our purposes, many evangelicals also hold to an understanding that adherence to the consensus position represents a first order issue of faithfulness to the gospel, meaning that those who depart from it or teach others to do so are stepping outside faithfulness to Christ. The reasons for this conviction as to the seriousness of disagreement over sexuality are complex and will be explored further throughout this book, but for now it is important to recognize that one of the ways in which the 'first order' nature of disagreement is signalled is by reference to the historic teaching of the church. Many evangelicals will state that the consensus position represents the unbroken tradition of the church, held to at least as long as the creeds themselves and departing from it therefore represents unfaithfulness.

In this chapter I explore the reasons why this argument cannot seriously be maintained. The tradition of the church has not historically held an unvarying stance towards sexuality that is the same as the evangelical consensus position, for the obvious reason that the consensus position is addressing a modern social situation (the decriminalization of homosexuality) by reference to modern understandings (the existence of people with a naturally occurring homosexual sexual orientation). This does not mean that the consensus position is wrong. Simply that it cannot be plausibly argued that this understanding had been set out in this way prior to the Seventies, even if it is argued that it is a legitimate development of earlier tradition. It is therefore misleading in the most basic sense to describe the consensus position as 'traditional' and more progressive understandings as 'revisionist'. Both conservative and progressive stances are to some extent revisionist. The characterization of current debate as being between those defending an unmodified historical tradition and those who are arguing for departure from it (which necessarily puts a high burden of proof on those arguing for change) is mistaken. Most Christians (and, in fact, most evangelicals) throughout history have not held to this position, stated in this way, on the basis of this interpretation of scripture, even if it is argued that the consensus position represents the most faithful reinterpretation of earlier tradition. Therefore, it cannot be argued that adherence to the consensus position is a first order issue of faith on the basis that it represents unbroken continuity with the traditional teaching of the church. It does not. Rather, it is a consensus that has existed among evangelicals since (at the earliest) the Seventies, and acts as a theological justification for a position of Anglican church policy originally argued for in the Fifties on different theological grounds.

Beyond this basic sense in which the consensus position is a modern understanding it is important to recognize that it also departs from earlier Christian tradition in several key areas. Most significantly the consensus position differs from earlier understandings in its insistence that a homosexual orientation is not sinful, and that homophobia is sinful and should be condemned. In fact, the consensus position differs from earlier tradition in a wide range of other areas too, but in its condemnation of homophobia it represents a clear and decisive break, adopting a moral stance that would have been incomprehensible to earlier tradition.

In this chapter I offer a fairly brief overview of pre-modern Christian teaching on sexuality, focusing mainly on understandings common in the pre-modern period around the establishment of the Church of England and the passing of the 1533 Buggery Act (after which point prohibition of same-sex acts became part of the law of the land and not a matter for church courts and theological debate). I will show that the church did indeed hold to an unvaryingly negative view of homosexuality, but that this was not expressed in the form of the evangelical consensus position. In the next chapter I will also demonstrate that the historic church did not draw on the same configuration of biblical texts to support its understanding. Having established that prior to the mid-twentieth century no one had set out the configuration of ethical approaches that form the evangelical consensus position, I will then explore the process by which it was formed, by tracing the history of British evangelical writing on the subject between the publication of Derrick Sherwin Bailey's *Homosexuality and the Western Christian Tradition* (widely recognized as the beginning of modern Christian ethical response to homosexuality) in

1955 and the most influential early statement of the consensus position in John Stott's *Issues Facing Christians Today* in 1984.

The tradition before 'the tradition'

1 Pre-modern Christians thinking about sex

The most obvious sense in which the consensus position differs from earlier tradition is that pre-modern understandings of sexuality did not include the modern category of 'homosexuality', and had no understanding of 'orientation', a point made forcefully by the evangelical scholar Richard Hays in regard to biblical interpretation: 'neither Paul nor anyone else in antiquity had a concept of "sexual orientation"', and supported by the majority of classical scholars.[3] Thus Marilyn Skinner notes that there is no term for sexuality in either Greek or Latin, and that Roman culture assigned sexual identity on the basis of people indulging in particular sexual practices, irrespective of the biological sex of those involved.[4]

It is important to belabour this point because modern evangelical scholars often put forward arguments that seem to downplay the significance of this. Thus the evangelical biblical scholar Robert Gagnon discusses ancient sources at length in order to establish that the idea of naturally occurring same-sex desire was known to at least some ancient philosophers.[5] However, the point he is making is not that the ancient world had a modern concept of sexual orientation, but that ancient writers condemned same sex acts in the awareness that some people might naturally be sexually attracted to members of their own sex. He is not making an argument that in the ancient world it would have made sense to describe a particular category of people as 'gay' in the way we might today, irrespective of whether they had acted on their desires or not. Rather, he is seeking to refute the idea that biblical prohibitions on same-sex activity can be disregarded because biblical writers were unaware of the possibility that some people might naturally experience same-sex desire. His argument is not that biblical authors understood the modern concept of orientation, but that *even if they had* they would have said the same thing, because they condemn same sex acts *irrespective* of whether they are in response to a natural desire.

This subtle distinction is often lost on modern evangelicals. The consensus position, which asserts strongly that no one should be condemned for their same-sex orientation and that homophobia is wrong, relies on a distinction that would be incomprehensible in the ancient world. The idea that it is meaningful to say that gay people are to be accepted and loved while also saying that same-sex sexual activity is to be rejected is almost incomprehensible from a pre-modern standpoint, where desire is discerned only in and through action. The consensus position frames church policy in relation to categories that literally make no sense outside the modern world. Attempting to trace lines of continuity to earlier Christian tradition therefore requires a process of translation to a degree that evangelicals tend not to recognize.

Obviously terms like 'pre-modern' are unhelpfully vague for most purposes, covering a vast swathe of history, but when it comes to discussing sexuality, modernity is a really significant point of discontinuity, even if we need to recognize its fuzzy edges, because of the way in which modern understandings and technology have radically transformed the way in which we think about sexuality. In modernity people started to think and talk about sexuality in radically different ways from how they had done before, because new technologies and cultural change opened up new possibilities. Modernity has brought legal equality between men and women, allowing women the freedom to choose a partner or to live independently. It has also brought widely available reliable contraception, for the first time completely separating sexual acts and procreation, making the conception of children an active choice on the part of sexual partners. It is important to recognize that the emergence of the concept of sexual orientation is also profoundly modern. This means that when in the twentieth century the church had to consider its policy around sexuality in response to decriminalization it was in a very real sense having to consider questions that it had never considered before, in that its own tradition of teaching on the subject had been largely unchanged for the last 400 years.

The idea that human beings possess an innate predisposition to experience sexual attraction either to members of the opposite sex, members of their own sex, or some point on a spectrum between the two (let alone that every point on this spectrum should be regarded as morally neutral rather than some being blameworthy), is a radically new and modern understanding. Although it is possible to point to the existence of non-pederastic same-sex relationships in the ancient world and to classical authors who discussed the possibility of a preference for same-sex adult partners, the overwhelming assumption of the classical Greek and Roman world was that these were (often shameful) oddities if indulged in. The prevailing view was that men (and by and large the literature of the ancient world has little interest in the sexuality of women) were capable of sexual attraction to either sex, that attraction to another man rather than an inferior female was understandable, but that nature and duty required a good citizen to produce children. Although gay people clearly existed in pre-modern times there is no real evidence that they were recognized as possessing a specific orientation and therefore being an identifiable group, and hardly any (outside of humorous stories or scandalous accusations) that their relationships were regarded by wider society as equivalent to marriage.[6] Before the concept of sexual orientation was developed in the nineteenth century, and the research done by Kinsey to demonstrate the prevalence of same-sex attraction in the twentieth there was no mental category in which 'gay people' could be placed. Without any concept of orientation or indeed of a gay person, the idea that you might affirm gay people as gay people while deploring their sexual behaviour becomes incomprehensible.

Pre-modern understandings of sexuality, because they lacked a concept of orientation, did not easily make the sort of sharp distinction between act and orientation that is basic to understanding the modern evangelical approach to condemning homophobia by affirming gay people while condemning gay sexual behaviour. It would be equivalent to going out of your way to affirm those consistently tempted to adultery. For a pre-modern Christian there are no 'gay people' to affirm. There are simply people, who are assumed to all be capable of experiencing desire towards both sexes. Desire directed towards your own sex is fruitless and therefore contrary to nature. There was a persistent tendency in pre-modern writings to associate desire towards one's own sex as an excessive form of 'natural lust' that throws off all normal constraints.[7] So a man lusting after another man is often regarded not as someone unable to lust after women, but more likely as someone whose natural lusts for women have been so overindulged that they are expressed in a form of indifferent lust that no longer troubles to make fine distinctions of gender. The fact that we are here dealing with an understanding of same-sex attraction that is radically different from a modern one is obvious.

It's hard to overstate the extent to which pre-modern approaches to sex and sexuality were structured around completely different conceptual categories than the ones we naturally use. To illustrate how this carried over into later periods than antiquity, I will delve in a little more detail into understandings of sexuality in Christian medieval Europe (the understandings that lay behind the Buggery Act). The work of the historian Ruth Mazo Karras makes clear that in medieval Europe, the modern idea of 'having sex' as an activity that two (or more) people of any combination of genders could logically engage in was simply not present. Sex was conceptualized around ideas of gender, and the significance of procreation and therefore penetration. Male and female experience of sex and sexual behaviour were understood in completely different ways. The proper sexual action was something done by a man to a woman, with their roles being distinctly different. Medieval Christian teaching about sex emphasized that sex was a duty for married couples, and took place primarily for procreation, not enjoyment (though there was a strong link made between spiritual devotion and abstinence from sex, and particularly devout couples might adopt an abstinent lifestyle by mutual consent once they were beyond childbearing years). Sex outside marriage was a sin (in fact some strands of teaching derived from Augustine suggested that feelings of sexual desire were sinful even in marriage, with the sacrament of marriage itself acting as absolution), but this was complicated by the fact that an unmarried couple having sex could be regarded as de facto having entered into marriage, thus legitimizing their having had sex. Promiscuity was in most cases not as significant an issue for the medieval church as adultery.[8]

I have dwelt in some detail on a few of the ways in which pre-modern Christian understandings of sex differed from our own to highlight the fact that the idea that 'the tradition of the church' in this area is an unchanging thing is fundamentally mistaken. When not just the culturally discernable options for behaviour but also the conceptual categories around sex, orientation and sexual behaviour change as significantly as they do over time, traditions have to change with them. A medieval Christian not only wouldn't express 'the traditional teaching of the church' in the same way we would, they couldn't do it. The concepts we use instinctively were not available to them. To faithfully transmit the tradition of the church through history is unavoidably an act of translation, involving choices about what terms and ideas are the 'best fit'. At times there will be several different options to consider. None of this means that the question, 'Is this the most valid way to express the inheritance of faith in our culture?' is not a meaningful question to ask. Rather, my point is that receiving the inheritance of faith requires us to ask that question. There is no 'innocent' reception of tradition that does not involve this sort of questioning.

2 Pre-modern Christians thinking about homosexuality

Having recognized some of the wider challenges involved in understanding what 'the tradition of the church on sex and relationships' means, I turn specifically to consider what the tradition of the church meant in regard to homosexuality. The strong connection of legitimate sex to procreation meant that non-procreative (fruitless) sexual acts were seen as especially sinful, as they went against the natural order. This was the category in which homosexual acts fell, therefore being far more serious than adultery or incest, which were sinful but 'natural'. For this reason Thomas Aquinas influentially declared that homosexual acts were the most serious sexual sin.[9]

This might sound like medieval Christians shared the same understanding as modern evangelicals. However, the degree to which this is not the case becomes instantly apparent once you realise that *all* fruitless sexual acts were viewed as unnatural in this way, meaning that masturbation or coitus interruptus might both legitimately be seen as 'unnatural' sexual sins, and far more serious than mere promiscuity or incest. When Henry VIII's Buggery Act made homosexual sexual acts a capital crime punishable by the state, the offence being punished was sodomy, the sin of Sodom, which was an offence defined by its nature as a non-procreative sexual act. It allowed prosecution for an act between two men, but also a man and a beast, or even a man and a woman (even if married). It had no application to most sexual acts between women. Some of these 'unnatural' sexual acts would be viewed as serious sins by modern evangelicals, and some might not be sins at all. This is because although medieval conceptions of what is 'natural' in sex revolve around procreation, modern evangelical conceptions (as we shall see) revolve around gender roles. Any serious attempt to defend the notion that modern evangelicals are simply inheritors of an unchanged tradition of teaching on sex and relationships therefore needs to take into account the huge significance of the largely unremarked modern evangelical acceptance of the legitimacy of contraception, which necessitated reinterpreting what constituted an unnatural sexual act in a way that did not revolve around procreation.

In fact, because medieval understandings of sexual acts arose in a highly patriarchal society, one of the ways in which medieval understandings differ most significantly from our own is that they were far more highly gendered and revolved around penetration. I have already noted that men's and women's experience of sex was understood to be completely different – because one penetrates and the other is penetrated. The consequences of this for conceptualizing homosexuality are significant. Although a male-male sexual act would easily be recognized as unnatural, involving a man placing another in the role of a woman, and their partner consenting to it, a female-female sexual act might not. There are very few records of prosecutions for same-sex acts between women, and those that exist tend to be focused around a penetrative act – a woman who was attempting to perform a 'male' sexual act.[10] In speaking of male same-sex acts as serious sins though not regarding them as more serious than other forms of sexual sin, evangelicals could broadly claim to be within the bounds of some earlier Christian tradition. However, in regarding female same-sex acts as equivalent in every way to male same-sex acts they are radically modifying it.

It is important to recognize the conceptual gap between modern and pre-modern Western understandings of homosexuality because it makes it very clear that there is no obvious univocal 'tradition' that can be drawn on in answering modern questions about homosexuality simply because what we now call 'homosexuality' is a modern concept. This is true in several key areas:

- There was no understanding of 'homosexual orientation' (the natural ordering of all people towards procreative acts was assumed).
- There was an understanding that any sexual act that prevented procreation from occurring was unnatural (so same-sex sexual acts, masturbation and contraception were all unnatural and sinful).

- There was no unified concept of a 'same-sex sexual act' (as all properly sexual acts were assumed to involve penetration or its possibility, same-sex acts between women were not regarded as equivalent to same-sex acts between men, indeed in some circumstances they may not have been regarded as sex acts at all).

Evangelicals and Christian tradition

It should by now be clear that the pre-modern Christian tradition of teaching on homosexuality could not simply be followed without serious need for reinterpretation when the Church of England began to seriously engage in reflection on the subject in the early twentieth century. Indeed, for the English church homosexuality had not been an area with any need for serious theological and ethical debate since the 1533 Buggery Act. In 1533 the Buggery Act was enacted as part of a package of Reformation legislation, removing sodomy from the jurisdiction of ecclesiastical courts, placing such cases under the authority of the crown, and in the process declaring them capital crimes. (It should be noted in passing that church courts had often not punished same-sex offences as severely.) Later reforms to the law would reduce this punishment to imprisonment, but occasioned little fresh ecclesiastical debate.

Modern evangelical rhetoric can give the impression that pre-modern Christians (and particularly evangelicals) held to approximately the same position in regard to homosexuality as an orientation as that held by modern evangelicals. However, this is far from being the case. The modern evangelical consensus position is radically different from earlier tradition. Christian tradition, in focusing more on action than orientation, did not and could not argue that gay people can be fully accepted into the church as long as they don't act on their desires, or that homophobia should be condemned. For much of its history, the church has actively made the case that gay people (identifiable only by means of their actions) are deserving of the most serious punishment, up to and including death. In some cases, including periods of church history often lauded by evangelicals such as Calvin's Geneva, the church has actively presided over executions of gay people. Christian tradition correspondingly does not regard homosexuality as less than God's perfect intention for humanity but not in itself sinful. Indeed some strands of Christian tradition have regarded all sexuality as sinful, with homosexuality (both act and desire) as among the most serious of sins. Christian tradition in the pre-modern era is for the most part profoundly homophobic by any meaningful standards.

In the nineteenth century, as evangelicals became politically influential and began to become more interested in public morality, campaigning on reform of laws around prostitution for the protection of children, they showed no interest in condemning homophobia. In fact, the 1885 Criminal Amendment Act, which notoriously replaced the prohibition of 'buggery' with a prohibition of 'gross indecency between men' (the move widely recognized as turning it into a blackmailer's charter by creating an offence with a severe penalty and an ambiguous definition), was passed by Parliament largely due to heavy lobbying by the Society for Prevention of Cruelty to Children, founded by the evangelical Lord Shaftesbury the year before. It can be argued that evangelicals had not intended this – the change to the law on homosexuality was due to a malicious and misunderstood amendment by Henry Labouchere MP (himself agnostic), but they certainly showed no concern over it. Unlike the stated position of modern evangelicals, there was little sense that they saw protecting gay people from persecution as a priority.

By the mid-twentieth century it was becoming very apparent that the new law on homosexual offences was so poorly written that it was open to abuse by the malicious, requiring little evidence and imposing severe penalties including devastating reputational damage on those found guilty (and often even those accused). Given the fact that modern understandings of sexuality were now suggesting that some men were simply gay through no fault of their own, and that the danger they posed to the stability of society was demonstrably less than adulterers (who committed no criminal acts), the Church of England was interested in supporting legal reform. This was the context in which Derrick Sherwin Bailey, then the church's leading expert on sexual ethics, published his *Homosexuality and the Western Christian Tradition* in 1955. It was the first serious work done on the biblical and historical aspects of homosexuality in the modern age, which essentially drew a line under earlier tradition and reinterpreted it for the modern age. As we shall see, evangelicals themselves did not start to produce much writing in the field until around 20 years later, by which time they were playing catch-up – seeking to offer a conservative corrective to an array of more liberal writing published in the Sixties.

This raises an obvious question. The historical facts of the situation are not really in dispute: the historical Christian tradition was radically different from any of the approaches to sexuality presented by modern Christians. Bailey set out the first modern Christian approach to homosexuality in the Fifties. In the Sixties a series of liberal authors began to explore radical departures from the position established by Bailey. In the Seventies evangelicals began writing about sexuality and relationships and by the Eighties these writings had been consolidated into a widely held consensus position that is now referred to as 'the historic teaching of the church'. Yet this position expressed in this way does not seem to appear like this anywhere prior to the mid-twentieth century. So where did it come from? And how did evangelicals come to think it was a simple restatement of the traditional teaching of the church? I will spend the rest of this chapter attempting to answer the first of these questions, and return to the second question in Chapter 3.

The rejection of homophobia

In understanding what separates modern and pre-modern responses to homosexuality, perhaps the single most important aspect is the rejection of homophobia. One reading of the significance of Bailey's work is to see it as the church moving towards a rejection of the homophobic aspects of tradition. This is not to suggest that Bailey's work itself was devoid of homophobia or that the Church of England even today is free of it. However, the debate around decriminalization in many respects was an unspoken debate around homophobia: was it right to single out gay sexual offences as subject to a level of prosecution and public shame out of proportion to the way any straight sexual offence was treated? The normalization of a rejection of homophobia among all sections of the modern church has been so complete by now that it is easy to pass over how swift a change this has been. However, no denunciation of homophobia would be found in any evangelical writing about sexuality prior to the mid-twentieth century, yet it was common in all the writings after it. For this reason the centrality of a rejection of homophobia to the earliest evangelical writing on sexuality in the Seventies demands comment.

At the beginning of the twentieth century, although the Church of England had been actively involved in the discussions around the decriminalization of homosexuality, evangelicals had not been part of these discussions. The early twentieth-century civil war between liberal and conservative evangelicals had led to what the historian David Bebbington calls 'The Great Reversal', where conservative evangelicals, previously highly active in issues of social justice, withdrew to focus more narrowly on evangelism until they chose to re-engage in the Sixties, under the leadership of John Stott. This meant that when evangelicals began to re-engage with church and world they were engaging with a debate the broad parameters of which had already been sketched out by Bailey's work, and which they largely accepted unquestioned, focusing more on critiquing his biblical exegesis.

Bailey's book challenged and repositioned the church in relation to earlier tradition. Bailey recognized that the earlier tradition of the church was unremittingly hostile towards gay people, and that this had distorted it in a way that made it erroneous and defective as a guide for current practice. For this reason a clear aim of his research was to demonstrate that this homophobia was not an inherent part of a Christian response to homosexuality, and that a modern Christian could regard gay people as worthy of love, acceptance and freedom from legal prosecution and oppression even if (as he argued) homosexual sexual acts were still regarded as sinful. He thus ended his book with a call for 'the education of the public to a sense of understanding and responsibility for the men and women who labour under this peculiar handicap, and the dissipation of prejudices and false ideas regarding the homosexual condition'.[11]

The fact that modern evangelicals are conscious of breaking with earlier tradition in rejecting homophobia was explicit in the earliest evangelical writings, even if more recent evangelical writing takes rejection of homophobia for granted. Early evangelical teaching has a clear concern to accept gay people, condemn homophobia and repent of the church's past. David Field in 1976 wrote:

> [The Christian can offer] a welcome for those whom society ostracizes; and a desire to educate both young inverts themselves and those among the heterosexual majority whose attitude towards homosexuals is compounded of suspicion and misunderstanding.[12]

Three years later, David Atkinson wrote:

> It is incumbent on the wider Christian fellowship to repent of its attitudes of rejection, and work at being the fellowship of support in which the summoning of practising homosexuals to repentance and change in their lifestyle ... can be made realistically in the context of warm and supportive charity, and not cold pharisaic legalism ... a recognition of [the fact that homosexuality is involuntary] ... should provoke sympathetic and caring responses rather than moralistic abhorrence or legalistic coercion.[13]

Finally, in 1984 in his first edition of *Issues Facing Christians Today*, John Stott noted frankly that 'love is just what the church has generally failed to show to homosexual people'.[14]

Inasmuch as they seek to distance themselves from a homophobic tradition, modern evangelicals are adopting a firmly revisionist position, and are followers of the modern tradition of Christian reflection on homosexuality that derives from Bailey. Modern evangelicals, however much they might decry modern liberal approaches to sexuality, are actually far closer to them than they are to a pre-modern Christian position. Although modern evangelicals might not agree with the sexual revolution and all that it brought with it, they mounted no sustained campaign for the recriminalization of homosexual activity. The conservative evangelical rhetoric that suggests they are simply defending a centuries-old tradition is therefore both misleading and dangerous, as it could imply that fundamentally they continue to stand in solidarity with a homophobic Christian tradition and feel that deviating from it is an act of faithlessness to the gospel.

Derrick Sherwin Bailey's *Homosexuality and the Western Christian Tradition*

To understand where the evangelical consensus position came from, it is important to understand the broad shape of Bailey's argument. Although evangelicals were later to explicitly distance themselves from it, decrying it as a piece of liberal scholarship, we have already seen that in one of its central arguments, the rejection of homophobia, they followed it closely. In fact, Bailey's work was so significant in reframing debate on sexuality that it was arguably not until the publication of the research of Gagnon in 2001 (effectively re-evaluating all the ancient texts that Bailey had examined) that evangelicals decisively moved away from referencing it. Bailey's work set the parameters for modern Christian debate on the subject, as well as providing the basis for the Church of England's official stance. Despite their critique of Bailey (and most of the evangelical authors who mention him explicitly critique him), it is important to recognize that the church policy position that evangelicals adopted towards homosexuality was essentially identical to the one he set out. In fact, when evangelicals think of themselves as defending the traditional teaching of the Church of England this is implicitly what they mean – they are defending the position of church policy advocated by Bailey in the Fifties, even if they explicitly reject most of the argument he set out to justify it.

Bailey's analysis in *Homosexuality and the Western Christian Tradition* is that the historical teaching of the church on homosexuality has been distorted by a disproportionate focus on the Sodom narrative of Genesis 19, a failure to recognize the existence of 'inverts' (that is, people with a fixed and exclusive same-sex orientation), a disproportionate focus on penetrative acts and on men. Because of this he argues that the tradition as a whole must be rejected. The misinterpretation of Genesis 19 created an understanding of homosexuality as a heinous act that brought judgement from God, and conflated it with ancient notions of out-of-control and violent lust that had no room to consider the possibility of gay people as a naturally occurring group whose orientation was unchosen and not subject to change. The dominance of this passage in the Christian imagination led to misinterpretation of all the other scriptural passages generally appealed to support the traditional teaching on homosexuality. All of those texts, when examined through the eyes of modern critical scholarship, were ultimately irrelevant to the modern debate on sexuality. In addition, the deep-rooted patriarchal nature of Christian tradition, being written by men largely for men, meant that all traditional discussion of sexuality was inextricably focused around male concerns. Female homosexuality was almost invisible in Christian tradition, and when homosexuality was discussed it was almost always exclusively focused on behaviour around penetration and concerned with men and masculinity. This meant that in discussing the modern questions around homosexual orientation, and same-sex sexual activity (regarded as the same sort of behaviour whether engaged in by men or women and whether it involved penetration or not) there was hardly anything in Christian tradition of direct relevance.

On this basis then, Bailey argued that the church needed to set aside all of the existing Christian tradition of teaching on homosexuality, and construct a new approach that started with its existing tradition of theology around heterosexual marriage and gender. This approach, that began by setting out heterosexuality and heterosexual marriage as the norm, naturally led to an understanding that homosexuality and gay relationships are a departure from that norm. Bailey's argument was that rather than viewing homosexuality as a morally blameworthy departure from the norm, as past Christian tradition had done, it should be understood as a disability. Like disability it is naturally occurring and prevents some people from experiencing sexual relationships as God intended. It is contrary to God's intention in creation, but in itself morally neutral, not sinful. This understanding opened the way for the church to robustly condemn homophobia. Gay people's inability to experience desire for members of the opposite sex should be cause for compassion rather than condemnation on the part of the church. He explicitly stated that homosexuality was not medically harmful and not linked to paedophilia. He further argued (effectively against the understanding of Aquinas that homosexual sin constituted the most heinous form of sexual sin) that gay sex was analogous to incest – it was entirely natural and good sexual desire that was wrongly directed. The nature of homosexual desire as normal human sexual desire, and the genuineness of the love was not to be doubted. Gay people love in exactly the same way as straight people.

This was as far as Bailey's revisionism took him. Having reset the theological understanding of homosexuality in such a way as to provide a robust basis for the condemnation of homophobia, he simply restated current church teaching on sexual relationships: the only permitted sexual relationship was heterosexual marriage and any departure from this was sin. However, the church does not insist that all sin is also a crime punishable by the state, and if there is evidence that criminalization is causing suffering to a particular group of people out of all proportion to any damage they might be doing to society then the church is right to call for decriminalization. He argued it was inconsistent for the church to argue that adultery should not be criminalized but gay sex should when indisputably adultery did far more damage to the fabric of society.

Having set out Bailey's approach, we should also recognize what he does not address. Writing when he did, with homosexuality still criminalized, it is perhaps unsurprising that Bailey gave no serious consideration to how the church might respond to questions raised by openly gay clergy or Christian same-sex couples seeking blessings or marriage, or wanting to adopt children. However, it is clear that the outlines of both modern conservative and progressive Christian responses that do address these questions can be traced back to and justified from his work. Conservatives have essentially maintained the same position explicitly set out in Bailey's work: homophobia is condemned, and heterosexual marriage is the only acceptable pattern of sexual relationship. Progressives, however, have developed his understanding of homosexuality as disability rather than sin in light of the changed cultural landscape since the Fifties: compassion for the disabled now legally includes making reasonable adjustments so that they can participate in society as fully as possible. That this includes the possibility of same-sex marriage and following a vocation into ministry seems simple common sense when such changes can be made with so little impact on anyone else (why should my marriage make yours any less valid?). In fact, as is the case with more radical theological understandings of disability, some progressives would go further in their understanding of homosexuality as disability: it is wrong and exclusionary to see the disabled as less than God's perfect intention in creation. Gay people are therefore to be viewed not as some sort of divine mistake or a second-class human being, but as expressive of God's perfect intention in creation. God intended them to be as they are, it is society that needs to change to accommodate them, not the other way round.

Understanding the general shape of Bailey's argument is therefore hugely important for understanding why modern debate is where it is. Bailey both is and is not the key source for both evangelical and liberal thought on the subject. The fact that liberals tend to acknowledge his influence, and evangelicals (if they mention him at all) tend to cast him as the grandfather of liberal approaches underlines his significance to both of them, and the divisive (and amnesiac) nature of the current debate.

Early responses to Bailey

These divergent responses to Bailey's resetting of Christian tradition rapidly made themselves felt. The explicit dominance of the rather cautious Church of England approach he represented did not long survive the passing of the Sexual Offences Act in 1967. The church had been heavily involved in the Campaign for Homosexual Equality, but this self-consciously establishment group had no desire to support more radical legal reform, and as the Sixties and Seventies progressed the loudest voices around gay rights became those of gay people themselves, finally able to have their existence publicly acknowledged. In wider society, this was expressed in the short-lived but influential Gay Liberation Front and in the more enduring Pride marches. In the church, voices calling for more radical moves towards acceptance, accompanied by a theology that sought to find positive examples of gay people in scripture and tradition, began to be heard. New ethical approaches that encouraged a focus on acting in a loving manner rather than adherence to set biblical commands began to be influential. John Robinson's *Honest to God* had sounded this note in 1963 and a broader argument for a new ethical approach was expressed in Joseph Fletcher's *Situational Ethics* published in 1966. In 1967 Normal Pittenger published *Time for Consent?* arguing for a far more tolerant and accepting attitude to gay people in the church. The American and gay-affirming Metropolitan Community Church established a study group in London in 1972. In 1976 the Gay Christian Movement was established as an ecumenical campaigning group. Its first president, Revd Peter

Elers conducted a service of blessing for a lesbian couple the following year. This started a steady stream of such services, either in churches or homes, many of which prompted outrage in the wider church, with GCM publishing orders of service for wider use from 1978. Internal debates within the GCM about the extent to which gay Christians sought to emulate heterosexual marriage and the extent to which they represented a challenge to such existing restrictive sexual norms and required a revolution in sexual ethics began to draw on new ethical thinking to justify new patterns of relationship, as with Norman Pittenger's 1978 GCM pamphlet *Some notes on an ethic for homosexuals*, which defined all sexual acts as good as long as they treated the other as a person not a thing. The sense that progressive gay Christians were seeking not simply to make a case for equality, but for a wholesale rewriting of sexual ethics in which marriage would no longer be the ideal and promiscuity might be celebrated, started to create serious alarm among conservatives in the wider church.[15]

Evangelicals did not immediately engage in this debate. Although combatting what they saw as the sinfulness of the permissive society (not least through movements such as the Nationwide Festival of Light) was an early priority for evangelical re-engagement with church and society, the Church of England's policy on sexuality (represented by Bailey) was one they supported, and radical groups like the Lesbian and Gay Christian Movement (as it soon became) were clearly not representative of the church as a whole. There was in fact an early growth in gay evangelical visibility, suggesting that in some places at least evangelical responses to gay people were marked primarily by a desire to reject homophobia. The Metropolitan Community Church itself was broadly evangelical. The LGCM established an evangelical fellowship. The earliest evangelical writings on the question of homosexuality did not focus on the need to defend a Christian orthodoxy. Instead, they were concerned primarily to address the pastoral issues faced by church leaders (assumed to be straight) in supporting gay Christians.

The pseudonymous *The Returns of Love* by 'Alex Davidson', published by InterVarsity Press in 1970 was possibly the first British evangelical publication on the subject of homosexuality. It was a first-hand account of a gay evangelical determined to live an abstinent life. It didn't make any attempt to address theological questions, simply taking for granted a conservative position, but its message of compassion and rejection of homophobia was influential on evangelical leaders, being cited both by Field and by Stott. It underlined the position established by Bailey, that homosexuality should be seen as analogous to disability and met with compassion not condemned as sinful: 'there really are men like us, with a certain peculiarity in our make-up which is in itself no more morally blameworthy than left-handedness'.[16] It was also clear that gay love is genuine love, that the feelings of attraction experienced by a gay person were exactly the same as those experienced by a straight person – entirely good and healthy feelings, simply wrongly directed. Although the book did nothing to increase the acceptance of gay people who failed to adopt an abstinent lifestyle, it clearly showed that a gay evangelical was not a contradiction in terms, indeed that they could be seen as an exemplary Christian.

By the Seventies there was a growing sense within the Church of England that the theological questions posed by sexuality needed fresh examination. Bailey's work had by now clearly been overtaken by events. This eventually led to the Gloucester Report, published as *Homosexual Relationships: A Contribution to Discussion* in 1980, which restated the same policy and interpretation of scripture as Bailey. However, this reaffirmation that scripture had nothing to contribute to modern debate was now causing disquiet among evangelicals. Evangelical members of the Board of Social Responsibility added a dissenting postscript to the Report, arguing strongly that theological justification for the church's current policy should be rooted in scripture and not in relativistic ethics. It was during the Seventies that evangelicals embarked on the creative and exploratory process of establishing an entirely new biblical theology of sexuality that would support the 'traditional position' as set out by Bailey. It is important to recognize that this is what evangelicals were doing, because neither conservatives nor progressives characterize it in this way. Conservatives (if they give any explicit acknowledgement to this as innovative scholarly work) tend to describe it in terms that suggest they were simply pointing out the clear underlying biblical theology that had been there all the time. They were not so much constructing a theology as archaeologically rediscovering it. Bailey would retrospectively become the liberal who had moved away from the earlier clear biblical tradition. Liberals on the other hand tend to present evangelicals as uncritically holding on to a pre-modern homophobic tradition, or (if they acknowledge the fact that evangelicals have clearly engaged in significant modern scholarly work in the area) aggressively seeking to steer the church in a more conservative direction. The reality is that evangelicals were simply seeking to maintain and defend the position established by Bailey in the Fifties (and upheld by the Church of England in 1980), yet provide it with a biblical justification that was more congenial to their own theological convictions. Their lived experience – that all they were doing was providing a robust defence for the position held by the Church of England in the face of pressing new challenges – explains why the conviction that they were simply restating the tradition of the church took hold so easily.

Towards the evangelical consensus position

The first serious ethical writing on the subject of homosexuality by a British evangelical was David Field's 1976 Grove booklet *The Homosexual Way – A Christian option?* Grove booklets, which had begun publication in 1971, with the ethics series beginning in 1973, were intended to function as a quick way of addressing topical issues from an evangelical viewpoint. Field's tone throughout is of one defending a received tradition against progressive excesses, with the implication that Bailey is the first and most significant of the liberal revisionists whose excesses must be resisted so that the traditional biblical understanding can be retained. Bailey's interpretation of scripture is thoroughly debunked, though the church policy positions he argued for – rejection of homophobia and heterosexual marriage as the only faithful pattern of sexually active life – are accepted without their source ever being acknowledged.

It is clear how much Field draws on Bailey, even in places where this is not explicitly acknowledged. He presents the reality of sexual orientation as a matter-of-fact statement of the best understanding of modern research, using Bailey's now outdated language of the distinction between pervert and invert. It should be noted that the acceptance as established fact that a certain proportion of people naturally experience attraction only to members of their own sex, which is basic to modern understandings of sexuality, is never seriously questioned by British evangelicals. Given later evangelical reluctance to allow scientific research to determine ethics (particularly in regard to the viability of various conversion treatments), this early and complete acceptance of the validity of Kinsey's work (itself only published in the Fifties) is remarkable, and seems to be due to the unacknowledged influence of Bailey. Having explicitly accepted a non-traditional understanding of variance in sexual orientation without argument, Field makes the case that although this is unchosen (and thus not blameworthy) in theological terms it is unnatural – a result of the Fall and not part of God's intention in creation. This is recognizably the same 'disability' understanding as that of Bailey, albeit presented in slightly different language. This pattern of explicit rejection and implicit acceptance of Bailey continues in Field's discussion of the Sodom narrative of Genesis 19. Field frankly recognizes that the passage is both central to earlier tradition and unhelpful in addressing modern questions around sexuality. However, this apparent acceptance of the central thrust of Bailey's argument is de-emphasized by the painstaking care taken to show that his detailed interpretation of the passage is wrong. Field thus presents his implicit acceptance of Bailey's argument that Genesis 19 is largely irrelevant as an explicit rejection of Bailey's liberal interpretation of the passage and the successful defence of a 'traditional' understanding of scripture.

In constructing a new biblical basis for the church's policy on sexuality, Field suggests that Romans 1 is the central text, because it roots condemnation of homosexual behaviour (but not orientation) in the doctrine of creation. Homosexual orientation is argued to be the result of the Fall, but not in itself morally wrong unless expressed in behaviour, which is sinful. Rather than homosexuality being understood as a chosen perversion of the created order, it is an unchosen 'inversion'. This does not change the fact that the only faithful lifestyles for the Christian disciple are heterosexual marriage or celibacy. Given that all this is done in a Grove booklet of 24 pages, and Field himself appears to have no consciousness that he is doing anything more radical than offering a defence of a well-established position, it is unlikely that Field is personally entirely responsible for this new framework of biblical interpretation. He is almost certainly drawing on a wider received unwritten tradition within evangelicalism that had developed over the 20 years since Bailey's work was published and the Church of England threw its weight behind decriminalization. Given the fact that the Sixties and Seventies were an enormously confident, fruitful and imaginative period for British evangelicalism this seems highly likely. Field's booklet therefore essentially represents a codification (and undoubtedly a rationalization, as Field himself was an ethics tutor at a theological college) of a pre-existing unwritten evangelical common mind on the subject.

As we will see, Field's work represents a key early move towards forming the evangelical consensus, but in some key respects is not entirely congruent with the consensus position as it would eventually emerge. The Seventies seem to have been a period where a degree of fluidity within evangelical understandings was still accepted, something that is demonstrated by comparison with some other influential publications by evangelical writers around the same time: John White's *Eros Defiled* and Roger Moss's *Christians and Homosexuality*. Moss's pastoral approach was cited approvingly by Stott in the second edition of his *Issues Facing Christians Today*, and Moss himself cites Field. White's book, although American, was published in a UK edition by InterVarsity Press. Like Field, they advocated sexual abstinence as the appropriate path for gay Christians, and their tone was deeply sympathetic to gay people and condemnatory towards the church's homophobic history. They directly challenged evangelicals to repent of homophobic attitudes and made it clear that church culture was too often hostile to gay people. They condemned the exclusion of gay people from church communities, with Moss going so far as to assert that a gay couple in a committed relationship should not be excluded from any aspect of church life, even if he would not himself commend the relationship. Moss in particular was more liberal than the later evangelical consensus position even in regard to his interpretation of scripture. He accepted Bailey's point that the Bible 'has not dealt with our question of homosexual relationships entered into freely with loving intent', and at one point even speculated that sincere Christians in committed homosexual relationships might be fulfilling God's will in an unexpected way, though his eventual conclusion was rather less radical.[17]

The need for an evangelical consensus

If there are some signs of a tolerance for a diversity of views among evangelicals in the Seventies there were clearly limits to this. Where (as Stott's support for Moss demonstrates) diversity in interpretation of scripture could be tolerated, diversity in advocacy of church policy could not. This became clear with the 1978 publication of Virginia Mollenkott and Letha Dawson Scanzoni's *Is the Homosexual My Neighbour?* in the US. This was the earliest and best-known example of a thoroughly pro-gay evangelical approach, from writers with a feminist outlook but impeccable evangelical credentials. Mollenkott was stylistic consultant for the New International Version of the Bible. They held strongly to the authority of scripture, were revisionist yet cautious, occasionally disputing more progressive interpretation of passages, yet argued like Bailey and Moss that scripture said nothing directly about those with a stable same-sex orientation seeking to enter a committed relationship, so that a moral stance must be constructed drawing on passages not directly addressing homosexuality. Unlike either of these, however, they advocated seeing same- and opposite-sex relationships as fully equivalent, with scripture pointing to a covenantal union between two people as the created pattern for human sexuality. There was no openness here to the liberal argument for a sexual ethics that allowed promiscuity. However, this sense that Mollenkott and Scanzoni were being responsible in interpreting scripture and moderate in the proposals they made was in itself very threatening to the emerging evangelical consensus position. Stott would explicitly refute Mollenkott and Scanzoni's argument in his discussion.

A second key text in the emergence of the evangelical consensus was David Atkinson's Latimer House publication *Homosexuals in the Christian Fellowship*, published in 1979. Although still brief, this was a far more substantial discussion than Field's Grove booklet. Atkinson adopted a far more carefully nuanced stance towards Bailey than Field. He rejected the pervert/invert distinction, preferring to acknowledge Kinsey's work on a continuum of sexuality in which all permutations naturally occur. He instead used the language of orientation and act – all are to be accepted regardless of orientation, with moral judgement coming on our actions rather than (and irrespective of) our predispositions.

Atkinson's basic theology of sexuality was more sophisticated than Field's, in that he made a key theological move in regard to the doctrine of creation that Field did not. For Atkinson, based on his reading of the creation narratives in Genesis, gender and the male-female sexual partnership of marriage made possible by it, was the only human difference that was part of God's perfect intention in creation. Although he does not acknowledge it, this is clearly an argument that can be traced back to Augustine, who argues that gender and thus the possibility of procreation was inherent in creation before the Fall. This point has two central implications. The first is that sexuality with all that it entails (sexual desire and acts) should be recognized as fully a part of God's perfect intention in creation. Atkinson frankly recognized the extent to which this represented a departure from tradition, but argued that this modern acceptance of the goodness of sexuality per se was truer to biblical ideals: 'this norm [that human sexuality is God's good intention in sexuality], let it be acknowledged, has not been central in traditional Christian attitudes to sexuality, which have often leaned harder on the negative approach of Augustine than on the more positive teaching of the biblical authors'.[18]

The second implication Atkinson drew out was that sexual orientation, unlike gender, was a point of human difference that was a result of the Fall and not intended by God. Although not sinful in itself, it made a place for sin. This was in many ways a simple rephrasing of Bailey's disability understanding, though explicitly rooted in a reading of Genesis, and strongly connected by contrast with gender. This meant that there was no possibility of a moral equivalence between heterosexual relationships and homosexual ones. One was part of God's perfect intention, the other an unintended consequence of the Fall.

This engagement with the creation narratives framed Atkinson's approach to the other biblical material. In general, Atkinson accepted Bailey's argument that none of the passages directly addressing homosexuality can be directly applied to modern questions, but disputed the implication that they therefore have no relevance. Instead he argued that broad principles within them can be discerned that continue to be applicable: in particular he found a consistent recognition that male-female one-flesh relationships are regarded as the norm and all departures from this are unacceptable (whether taking the form of adultery or same-sex relationships). He offered a substantial reinterpretation of the Levitical texts on this basis to make a case that they follow an underlying moral logic that sees the prohibition of adultery as necessarily implying the prohibition of homosexual acts.

Finally, Atkinson made the case that (contrary to Bailey's argument) the idea of a naturally occurring disposition towards desire for your own gender was known in the ancient world, and therefore biblical authors wrote with the awareness of something akin to the concept of sexual orientation. Perhaps recognizing the weakness of this argument, he further argued that as the biblical texts focus on behaviour rather than the underlying dispositions behind them, they could not be ruled irrelevant in the light of modern understandings of orientation. On this basis Atkinson argued strongly that both homophobia *and* acceptance of homosexual relationships as non-sinful should be seen as wrong, developing a striking parallelism between the church and the gay believer who both needed to be willing to repent of past wrongdoing and commit to transformation of life.

Atkinson's work, like Field, established the continued relevance of the biblical material, albeit in a slightly different configuration. The stress was less on Romans 1 and more on an underlying one-flesh theology of male-female relationships inherent in all the texts. This emphasis in evangelical biblical theology was very clearly a key one for the formation of the consensus position, being explicitly drawn on by Stott. It is notable that in certain respects Atkinson left the door open for a more progressive position than all of this might suggest, highlighting the need to respect those Christians who in good conscience make different choices. At this point, however, his biggest influence on the developing evangelical consensus came through the prominence he gave to the doctrine of creation.

Issues Facing Christians Today – the codification of consensus

The evangelical consensus whose groundwork had been laid out in Field and particularly in Atkinson was to have its decisive expression in John Stott's *Issues Facing Christians Today*. Despite the fact that clear lines of continuity can be drawn between these works it should be noted that Stott was a distinctive voice in his own right. His discussion did not by any means represent a simple adoption of the ideas of others. Stott was a key figure in global evangelicalism throughout the second half of the twentieth century, calling for evangelicals to confidently engage with church and society rather than withdrawing from them. His *Issues Facing Christians Today*, first published in 1984, was one of the most important expressions of this commitment, discussing topics in the public eye, presenting a biblically based perspective, and in many cases encouraging his readers to become activists in the area, applying their faith to daily life, politics and the world of work. The book has had an enduring influence, continuously in print since its publication, and is now in its fourth edition.

The popularity of Stott's writing is in part due to its reasonableness and accessibility. Although discussing politicized issues his tone was never shrill, and he generally spoke from the centre ground of evangelicalism. In broad terms his approach is the same as that of Field and Atkinson. He affirmed the church policy position set out by Bailey (which by then had been restated in the Church of England's Gloucester Report) and accepted that the modern question of homosexuality cannot be addressed by directly applying the biblical texts explicitly discussing homosexuality. Like the other evangelical writers before him he critiqued the details of Bailey's biblical interpretation, and believed the texts still have some relevance as a 'negative witness'.

The area where Stott's contribution was truly distinctive was in the way he developed Bailey's move towards addressing the ethics of homosexuality as an implication of the theology of marriage by combining it with Atkinson's biblical theology of the place of gender in the doctrine of creation. In a detailed analysis of Genesis 2 he argued that God intended sex to be an act of one-flesh reunion of two beings, a man and a woman, who were once one. This approach to sexuality allowed Stott to argue that homosexual sexual acts are wrong because they are a sexual act outside marriage, just like adultery. He does not highlight the significance of this, but his argument is a highly distinctive shift away from a pre-modern Christian tradition that saw homosexual acts as unnatural because they prevent procreation, towards a modern evangelical tradition that saw them as unnatural because they undermined the created distinctiveness of gender. This is the key theological move that makes acceptance of the morally neutral status of contraception possible.

Although Stott writes in a pastorally sensitive manner, and shows little sign of homophobia himself (in fact he goes out of his way to affirm the pastoral insights of liberal gay writers), there are aspects of the way he condemns homophobia and discusses the pastoral needs of gay people that would have a more negative impact in the long term. Stott's rejection of homophobia seems sincere, however he does this by denying the validity of a gay identity: 'There is no such phenomenon as "a homosexual". There are only people, human persons, made in the image and likeness of God, yet fallen, with all the glory and the tragedy which that paradox implies.'[19] This point appears to be the root of the later recurrent tendency in more conservative evangelical circles for the use of 'same-sex attracted' as an identifier, and the ostentatious denunciation of 'gay' as an identity. Although well-meant, this has at times been heard as a homophobic denial of the very existence of gay evangelicals.

The other fateful aspect of Stott's discussion is his use of the work of the psychoanalyst Elizabeth Moberly. Moberly argued that homosexuality resulted from childhood trauma, encouraged the development of intrinsically unfulfilling relationships, and could be cured. In accepting her conclusions, Stott influenced a whole generation of evangelicals to adopt a basic approach to gay Christians that saw homosexuality as a disorder that might be open to the possibility of cure, and fundamentally believed that in advocating abstinence they were preventing the development of intrinsically unfulfilling relationships.

The creation of the evangelical consensus position as the invention of a Christian tradition

It is clear from the above that the evangelical consensus position, as expressed in Stott's *Issues Facing Christians Today* is a revisionist development of earlier pre-modern Christian tradition. It represents a newly affirming stance towards homosexuality, on the basis of a new interpretation of scripture, drawing on different passages, and building on a revisionist understanding of Christian sexuality and marriage.

Evangelicals first began responding to the modern question of homosexuality in the Seventies. After a formative period in which some of Bailey's hermeneutical conclusions were still accepted, the consensus position was set out clearly by Stott in 1984. The development of the consensus position was a part of the wider movement of evangelical re-engagement with church and society that began with the Keele conference of 1967. Keele represented a commitment to the place of evangelicals within a church that had Bailey's work as its foundational understanding of sexuality. Even if they disagreed with much of Bailey's argument (and they did), the commitment to remain within the Church of England meant tacitly accepting that they did not see this as incompatible with being evangelical Anglicans. By default then, Bailey's work became 'the tradition of the church' which they would from then on seek to defend against a liberal drift into more permissive understandings. Early evangelical writings make it clear that there is a consciousness that the position they are defending is different from earlier homophobic tradition, which they express repentance for. It is in defending the 'traditional' teaching of the church represented by Bailey from attempts to move in a more progressive direction that evangelicals start to critique his use of scripture, retrospectively giving the impression that rather than the creator of the new orthodoxy he is the forerunner of the liberals they are defending his position against.

Stott's statement of a consensus position retrospectively draws a line under a period of fluidity in exploring different evangelical approaches to sexuality as evangelicals start to consolidate around a single shared understanding. It is clear that what Stott's work represents is a modern biblical ethic. It is not simply a restating of tradition. It is not a proof-texting application of Bible passages. It represents significant interpretative work, drawing on multiple scholars, involving a discussion of a variety of individual passages, none of which directly address the modern issue of same-sex partnerships, and interpreting all of them in the light of ancient texts, the subsequent teaching of the church, and the broad message of scripture. The position it seeks to make a case for is the policy first advocated by Bailey, supported by the biblical arguments first offered by Field and Atkinson.

The evangelical consensus position on sexuality, often presented by conservatives as 'the tradition of the church' is in fact of twentieth-century origins. The only way it can be argued that the consensus position is substantially a restatement of earlier tradition or earlier interpretation of scripture is to implicitly assert that the rejection of homophobia is a relatively minor modification of that tradition, and that the traditional pattern of biblical interpretation is irrelevant to the tradition. The consensus position not only rejects homophobia, it also rejects an interpretation of scripture centred on the Sodom narrative and God's judgement on non-procreative sex as the sin against nature. These are not minor modifications to tradition, but represent a far-reaching modernization of that tradition.

It is inarguable that in its current form the consensus position did not exist before the Seventies, and there is no evidence that the pattern of biblical interpretation on which it is based was widely accepted in the Church of England before 1991, with the publication of *Issues in Human Sexuality*. Prior to this point, the understanding of Bailey (that no biblical texts could be seen as having direct relevance to the modern discussion) was still the official position of the Church of England, with *Homosexual Relationships* concluding in 1979 that 'The appeal to scripture ... provides us with a rather narrow and somewhat ambiguous base for contemporary Christian teaching.'[20] As we have seen, the consensus position is neither in line with traditional interpretation of scripture in regard to sexuality, nor in line with the understanding of scripture in pre-1991 Church of England reports. It can only realistically claim to have achieved broad acceptance within the Church of England within the last 30 years.

Having established what the actual origins of the consensus position are, in the next chapter I turn to examining the history of modern evangelical interpretation of the key biblical passages, to demonstrate that modern evangelical understandings rest on modern scholarship rather than on Christian tradition, and that there is still debate between evangelical scholars as to how they are to be interpreted.

Notes

1 Harrison, Glynn, 2016, *A Better Story*, London: InterVarsity Press, pp. xiv–v.

2 Harrison, 2016, p. 89.

3 Hays, Richard, 1996, *The Moral Vision of the New Testament*, Edinburgh: T&T Clark, p. 388.

4 Skinner, Marilyn B., 2014, *Sexuality in Greek and Roman Culture*, 2nd edn, Chichester: Wiley Blackwell, pp. 3–4, 21.

5 Gagnon, Robert A. J., 2001, *The Bible and Homosexual Practice*, Nashville: Abingdon Press, pp. 380–95.

6 See Williams, Craig A., 2010, *Roman Homosexuality*, 2nd edn, Oxford: Oxford University Press.

7 See here Gagnon's discussion in Gagnon, 2001, pp. 380–6.

8 Mazo Karras, Ruth, 2017, *Sexuality in Medieval Europe*, 3rd edn, Abingdon: Routledge.

9 Aquinas, Thomas, *Commentary on Romans*, in Rogers, Eugene F., 2002, *Theology and Sexuality*, Oxford: Blackwell, p. 106.

10 See Karras, 2017, pp. 148–55.

11 Bailey, Derrick Sherwin, 1955, *Homosexuality and the Western Christian Tradition*, London: Longmans, p. 176.

12 Field, David, 1976, *The Homosexual Way*, Bramcote: Grove Books, p. 23.

13 Atkinson, David, 1979, *Homosexuals in the Christian Fellowship*, Grand Rapids: Eerdmans, p. 118.

14 Stott, John, 1984, *Issues Facing Christians Today*, Basingstoke: Marshall, Morgan & Scott, p. 320.

15 Gill, Sean, ed., 1998, *The Lesbian & Gay Christian Movement*, London: Cassell.

16 Davidson, Alex, 1970, *The Returns of Love*, Westmont, IL: InterVarsity Press, p. 40.

17 Moss, Roger, 1977, *Christians and Homosexuality*, Exeter: Paternoster Press, pp. 28–32.

18 Atkinson, 1979, pp. 71–2.

19 Stott, 1984, p. 301.

20 Board for Social Responsibility, 1979, *Homosexual Relationships*, p. 39.

2

Evangelicals talking about scripture

In 2022, as the Church of England's General Synod approached its debate on the Living in Love and Faith material, Steven Croft, the evangelical Bishop of Oxford, released a book outlining his own journey from a conservative to a progressive position on sexuality, urging the church to similarly change its policy. Among the many responses was a pre-prepared and carefully considered response from Vaughan Roberts, vicar of St Ebbe's in Oxford, and therefore one of the most prominent conservative evangelicals in the diocese. His response respectfully disagreed, pointing particularly to what he saw as the key fault in Croft's response – his turning away from the clear sense of scripture to be swayed by personal experience or the influence of wider culture. Roberts summarizes this clear sense of scripture thus: 'Scripture affirms the goodness of sex within heterosexual marriage and forbids it in every other context.'[1] Going through all the individual texts addressing homosexuality as well as discussing the broader theme of biblical teaching on marriage, Roberts made a case that scripture was so clear that, 'In this particular clash between the contested "truth" claims of Scripture and contemporary culture, it appears that the Bishop wants us to preference the latter.'[2]

This sort of rhetoric has become a commonplace of evangelical discussion, which often gives the impression in regard to sexuality that there is a transparently clear meaning of scripture communicated in a well-known selection of passages that has been held to consistently by the church, and which liberals are instead turning their backs on and being swayed by the world around them. As we have already seen, at least one aspect of this is untrue – because of the disjunction between modern and pre-modern approaches to homosexuality, the church historically necessarily held to a different understanding of sexuality, and therefore would have read the witness of scripture differently. However, it is important to also consider more specifically the passages and pattern of interpretation advanced by the historic church and by evangelicals today. This raises a number of related questions. Has the church always discussed sexuality by reference to the same key texts? Can these texts be directly applied to a modern understanding of same-sex relationships? Are the key texts ones where it is possible to interpret them as condemning same-sex activity while also affirming those experiencing same-sex desire? Is the modern evangelical pattern of interpretation, which tends to approach questions of sexuality via a theology of marriage rooted in a particular reading of the creation narratives in Genesis, one found in pre-modern Christian tradition?

We have already established in Chapter 1 that the modern evangelical pattern of interpretation has taken a while to consolidate itself, and that in key respects this is because of the difficulties involved in disentangling the tradition of the church from homophobia. In this chapter I explore the way in which modern evangelical interpretations of the key passages of scripture that directly discuss homosexuality (Genesis 19; various references to *qadhesh* in Deuteronomy and 1 Kings; Leviticus 18.22 and 20.3; Romans 1; 1 Corinthians 6.9–10, and 1 Timothy 1.9–10) have developed during the twentieth century. I will also examine Genesis 1 and 2, which as we have seen have become central texts in evangelical interpretation since the Seventies. I will demonstrate that despite popular-level evangelical assertions that scripture is crystal clear, with the implication being that there are no thorny questions of interpretation with which to wrestle, conservative evangelical scholars have in the past (and in many cases still do) offered multiple different interpretations of all these passages. Key aspects of the modern evangelical pattern of interpretation, far from representing a clear understanding that has always been held by the church, rely on works of twentieth-century biblical scholarship that were unavailable to the early church. To demonstrate this, I will also explore some of the vastly different ways in which the early church understood and applied some of these passages.

It is important to point out, however, that none of this should be read as implying that modern evangelical interpretation of scripture is necessarily wrong. In fact, as my analysis will demonstrate, it is clear that modern evangelical biblical scholarship is frequently a helpful corrective to a misleading and homophobic early church tradition. Modern evangelical interpretation of these passages on the whole represents a high level of critical biblical scholarship that deserves a serious hearing. My intention in this chapter is not in any way to malign or throw doubt on the integrity of evangelical interpretation of scripture. My intention is, if anything, the opposite – to draw attention to the substantial body of modern evangelical scholarship in these areas, which should not be dismissed as amounting to little more than stating the crystal clear meaning of scripture. Pretending that what amounts to decades of hard work by evangelical scholars in studying, interpreting and weighing up of the best reading of different passages has not had to happen, and that anyone can open the Bible and clearly read the evangelical understanding straight off its pages helps no one. It simply plays into a rhetorical preference on the part of modern evangelicals to downplay the significance of their own serious engagement with critical scholarship in favour of talking about 'the plain meaning of scripture'. This anti-intellectualism does not serve either evangelicals or the wider church well. Evangelicals have done some significant scholarly work on sexuality over the last 50 years. Pretending that they haven't encourages liberals to write them off as fundamentalist literalists, and discourages evangelical lay people from doing the hard work that their tradition is capable of in engaging with the serious questions of today.

The Sodom narrative (Genesis 19)

The story of Sodom details the way in which the angelic visitors to Sodom (assumed by everyone to be men) who are offered shelter by Lot are threatened with gang rape by the lawless men of the city. This functions in the story as evidence of the depravity of the city on which God will bring destruction. The first thing to note in regard to the Sodom narrative is that it was far more central to pre-modern approaches to sexuality than it is to modern ones. Bailey noted that Genesis 19 was the single most influential text for pre-modern Christian understandings of homosexuality, listing over 20 different references to the sin of Sodom among the church fathers. A typical example here would be Augustine's reference to Genesis 19 in his *Confessions*:

> Therefore shameful acts which are contrary to nature, such as the acts of the Sodomites, are everywhere and always to be detested and punished ... Indeed the social bond which should exist between God and us is violated when the nature of which he is the author is polluted by a perversion of sexual desire.[3]

Same-sex offences were conventionally defined by reference to Sodom and the judgement of God that came upon them there – they were signs of a society standing under the judgement of God. The canons of the Third Lateran Council in 1179 condemn 'that unnatural vice for which the wrath of God came down upon the sons of disobedience and burned the five cities with fire'.[4] In law, 'sodomy' became one of the most commonplace ways of referring to homosexual offences, with the earliest documents of English law, the Fleta and Britton (originating from the court of Edward I) both using the term 'sodomite'. The link between homosexuality and the judgement of God on society meant that Genesis 19 was closely linked in pre-modern understanding to Romans 1, where homosexuality and a turning away from natural desire is described as a symptom of Gentile rejection of God and coming under his judgement. So in pre-modern biblical interpretation, Genesis 19 became the key text, often referred to when interpreting other texts. As we shall see, Aquinas does exactly this in his commentary on Romans 1.

The centrality of Genesis 19 was set aside decisively by Bailey in his 1955 analysis of the texts on homosexuality. Bailey's argument was that Genesis 19 had been completely misunderstood by pre-modern Christian writers, following a tradition that started in the intertestamental *Testament of Naphtali* (which clearly influenced Jude 7 and 2 Peter 2.4-8). This was so central to earlier understandings that it effectively rendered the bulk of the traditional pattern of scriptural interpretation useless. Part of this argument, as we have seen, rested on his analysis of the ways in which pre-modern understandings of sexuality were deficient. However, in addition, Bailey advanced some specific exegetical arguments about Genesis 19 to make the case it was fundamentally unconcerned with homosexuality. His argument was that the verb *yadha* 'to know', is only very rarely translated in a way that has a sexual reference. For Bailey, therefore, the men of Sodom were not demanding to rape the angelic visitors, but rather to check their credentials. Their offence was not a sexual one, but a violation of the ancient custom of hospitality.[5]

Modern evangelical scholars (in common with most modern scholars since) disagreed with Bailey's interpretation of the passage, feeling certain that *yadha* should be understood as having a sexual referent when used by the men of Sodom, given that it seemed unlikely that it did not have a sexual referent when used later in Lot's offer to give his daughters to the men. This point was made by both Field (1976) and Atkinson (1979).[6] However, they both also noted that as the story was about threatened sexual assault it could not be directly applied to loving and consensual relationships. These points were repeated in the Church of England report *Homosexual Relationships* in 1979 and repeated in *Issues in Human Sexuality* in 1991 and then in *Some Issues in Human Sexuality* in 2003, effectively becoming the Church of England's consensus on the interpretation of the passage.[7]

This evaluation of Genesis 19 was held by the majority of evangelical writers on the subject until recently. Moss (1977), Schmidt (1995), Bonnington and Fyall (1996) and Hays (1996) all adopt substantially the same interpretation as *Issues in Human Sexuality* (1991), joining a considerable scholarly consensus, including among evangelical biblical scholars, that Genesis 19 was concerned with sexual assault and therefore irrelevant to modern debate.[8] In Stott's first edition of *Issues Facing Christians Today* (1984) he appears to tacitly support the position that Genesis 19 has no relevance to modern debate, basing his understanding of homosexuality on other texts. This section was unchanged in the second and third editions. In the fourth edition in 2006, however, Stott's discussion of Genesis 19 changed, arguing that it was the homosexual nature of the offence rather than the rape that made the men of Sodom particularly blameworthy, citing the influence of the evangelical biblical scholar Gagnon, whose 2001 *The Bible and Homosexual Practice: Texts and Hermeneutics* had become the standard work of evangelical biblical scholarship on the subject.[9]

The degree to which Gagnon's 2001 work, supported by Davidson 2007, had changed the conservative evangelical interpretation of Genesis 19 is demonstrated not only by the change in Stott (2006), but also by the difference between Bonnington and Fyall's 1998 Grove booklet and Ian Paul's 2014 one. Although Bonnington and Fyall suggest that homosexuality may be the primary offence, they acknowledge 'There is a growing consensus about Genesis 19.1–29 that "Sodom is not about sodomy".'[10] Sixteen years later, Ian Paul characterizes this as the 'revisionist reading', with the 'traditionalist reading' of the passage being that same-sex sexual activity is the depth of depravity and deserving of God's judgement.[11] He offers no discussion of where scholarly consensus might lie in regard to these readings.

Gagnon's argument was that a binary opposition of gender, creating a male-female complementarity rooted in creation, lay behind all biblical prohibitions of homosexual activity, and was consistently presented as especially offensive to God. This meant that the same-sex nature of the offence, far more than this being threatened sexual assault, was the most significant element. In advancing this argument, Gagnon recognizes that he is disagreeing with the interpretations of other biblical scholars, including evangelicals holding to a conservative position. He explicitly critiques Hays (1996), who had argued (in line with most biblical scholars) that Genesis 19 is irrelevant to the modern debate around consensual same sex relationships.[12]

Davidson's argument is based on the meaning of *yadha* – he argues that *yadha* is not a term elsewhere used to indicate rape, which is always described with terms that have a connotation of force, and the fact that the same word is used to indicate the threat of the men of Sodom as is used for Lot's offer of his daughters means that a softer reading ('we want to have sex with'/'why don't you have sex with') is more appropriate.[13] This would suggest that the telling of the story deliberately de-emphasizes the element of non-consent involved in order to emphasize the element of same-sex desire. As we will see, Gagnon's work has had a significant impact on evangelical interpretation of all the key biblical texts, but in regard to Genesis 19 his influence, supported by Davidson, appears to have been to move the consensus of conservative evangelical opinion further away from the broader Church of England position held to in *Issues in Human Sexuality*. Self-evidently, given that the threatened rape does not occur, Gagnon and Davidson's interpretations highlight the extent to which homosexual desire, and not simply homosexual acts, are to be considered offensive to God.

In conclusion, pre-modern readings of Genesis 19 interpret it as the key text in condemning homosexuality, understood as both desire and action. Although most scholars disagreed with Bailey's non-sexual interpretation, there was broad acceptance of his judgement that the passage was irrelevant to the modern sexuality debate. After 2001, the work of Gagnon, supported by Davidson, has influenced some conservative evangelicals to depart from this scholarly consensus in asserting the continued relevance of Genesis 19 to modern debate on the basis that the men of Sodom are condemned primarily for the homosexual desire expressed in their offence. There is still no consensus among evangelicals on this interpretation of the passage. The Evangelical Alliance's *Biblical and Pastoral Responses to Homosexuality*, published in 2012, asserts that the intended act here is gang rape and this makes the passage less relevant to the modern debate.[14]

Old Testament references to male shrine prostitutes (Deuteronomy 23.17–18; 1 Kings 14.22–24; 1 Kings 15.12; 1 Kings 22.46; 2 Kings 23.7)

The Hebrew term *qadhesh*, which appears in scattered incidental references in the Old Testament, suggests the widely known presence of a class of people within Israel that come under God's judgement. Pre-modern interpretation was unanimous in associating the term with homosexual offenders. The Latin vulgate rendered *qadhesh* variously as *scortator* (fornicator) or *effeminatus* (male homosexual prostitute). This was then rendered 'sodomite' in the English authorized version. By the turn of the twentieth century the work of the anthropologist Edvard Westermarck was influential in understanding these references as suggesting the presence in Israel of male shrine prostitutes, with whom Israelite men involved in idolatrous worship of the gods of the surrounding nations would engage in ritual sex. However, the Septuagint does not translate *qadhesh* in a consistent way, and does not use terms that suggest homosexuality. The Hebrew *qadhesh* literally means 'consecrated one', and seems to refer to some sort of temple servant, whose female counterpart was the *qedheshah* of Deuteronomy 23.17–18.[15]

Bailey, in his study of Christian biblical interpretation, classified all of these as passages that did not have any direct reference to homosexuality and whose application was entirely due to mistranslation. He argued that there was no reason to believe that homosexual shrine prostitutes ever existed in Israel or the surrounding nations. Although he did not deny that acting as a religious prostitute was one of the duties of both the *qadhesh* and *qedheshah* he argued it was far more likely that in fertility cults, which many of these were, the sexual services provided were heterosexual. Therefore all these passages could be considered irrelevant for the modern debate.[16] It is notable that Bailey's judgement that these passages have no direct reference to the modern debate on homosexuality was until recently accepted by all sides, and most still make little use of them. Those passages referring to *qadhesh* have generally not been discussed in overviews of the relevant biblical passages by those presenting either a conservative or progressive reading.

Bailey's judgement that the *qadhesh* were not homosexual shrine prostitutes has been called into question more recently. Gagnon (2001) argued that the *qadhesh* unambiguously should be understood as male homosexual shrine prostitutes, a position accepted by Paul (2014), but which is disputed by *Some Issues in Human Sexuality* (2006), which explicitly notes that most scholars, even conservative ones, disagree with Gagnon on this point.[17] Stott argues that there is no evidence that the *qadhesh* engaged in same sex acts, a position he maintained in 2004 despite accepting Gagnon's interpretations of other passages.[18] Gagnon's argument that the references to *qadhesh* should be understood as references to male homosexual prostitutes is not a major part of his overall argument, simply acting to further support his overall point that prohibitions on homosexual acts are deep-rooted in Israel's understanding of a binary human sexual nature. Gagnon is the central scholar in a re-evaluation of the historical setting as one in which homosexual cultic prostitution was the most acceptable form of homosexual act in the Ancient Near East. Gagnon argues (contrary to Bailey's assumption that it is more likely that *qadhesh* provided heteroesexual services) that there is no evidence anywhere in the Ancient Near East for male cultic prostitutes doing this – they are only ever found offering homosexual services. Some of Gagnon's argument for the *qadhesh* as male homosexual shrine prostitutes has since been supported by Davidson (2014).[19] However, the *qadhesh* passages are generally still not discussed in detail except as deep background for interpreting the Levitical prohibitions on same sex acts (for example, Paul (2014)) suggesting that even for those holding to Gagnon's interpretation these are still not generally regarded as central texts.

In conclusion, although prior to modern discussion these passages were routinely understood as clearly referring to same-sex sexual practice (with *qadhesh* being translated 'sodomite'), modern scholarship beginning with Bailey has on the whole rejected this. The presumption that these texts are therefore not directly relevant to debate on the modern question of sexuality has generally been accepted by modern evangelicals. More recent scholarship from Gagnon and Davidson appears to be suggesting that they may still have relevance, but this has as yet not impacted most conservative evangelical discussion of the biblical material and they remain marginal.

Old Testament law (Leviticus 18.22 and 20.13)

These two texts are some of the most well-known biblical condemnations of homosexuality, taking the form of commandments that men lying with men as they would with women be put to death. These condemnations of male homosexuality in the Old Testament law were read straightfowardly in pre-modern biblical interpretation, and offered justification for capital punishment to be applied to homosexual offences, though they tended not to be given as much prominence as the Sodom narrative in theological discussion of homosexuality. The same assumptions we noted in early twentieth-century scholarship that led *qadhesh* to be understood as referring to male shrine prostitutes led to the widespread assumption that the homosexual acts condemned here were a part of the worship of the surrounding nations, and were therefore ultimately condemnations of idolatrous worship. Bailey argued by contrast that these passages should be read as referring to normal homosexual acts which would be regarded as detestable in their own right, rather than as referring to a well-known practice of ritual sexual acts which he denied existed, but noted that there was little evidence they were much enforced.[20] His argument was that this section of the law was in fact a piece of carefully crafted rhetoric, designed to convince the people of Israel to distance themselves from the surrounding nations who were assumed to be engaged in detestable (but not ritual) sexual practices. In attributing homosexual acts to the surrounding nations, the law was not so much attempting to accurately describe them as it was to convince the people that the nations were sinful and should be avoided. References to homosexual acts, which the people of Israel would see as sinful and repellent, therefore functioned as political slanders to reinforce the desired impression of the surrounding nations, and Bailey regarded them as having no relevance to discussions of modern sexuality.

Debate over whether these laws should be read as referring primarily to cultic sexual activity or as non-cultic sexual acts would continue at a popular level through the second half of the twentieth century, in part because of the common Protestant convention of distinguishing between non-binding religious and still-valid moral law. Hays (1996) is typical of more critically aware evangelical scholarship in rejecting this neat distinction.[21] Increasingly, debate became centred on attempts to discern an underlying logic behind the Levitical holiness code to help discern its ongoing relevance.

The anthropologist Mary Douglas's influential *Purity and Danger* (1966) offered an interpretation of the Levitical holiness code as centred around an idea of preserving purity and completeness, necessitating that mixing of kinds be avoided. Thus a man acting as a woman is mixing two kinds (male and female), which associates the prohibition with similar prohibitions against mixing of fabrics, crossdressing and incest. This analysis would be taken further by Countryman in *Dirt, Greed and Sex* (1988), which suggested that the law was best interpreted as attempting to regulate both property rights and ritual purity.[22] Douglas and Countryman would both be influential on progressive approaches, as offering an interpretation that suggested the Levitical texts operated on a basis that was irrelevant to the modern sexuality debate. The work of Douglas is thus still referenced in work as recent as Brownson (2013). By contrast, conservative interpreters like Atkinson (1979), attempted to suggest an underlying logic that remained relevant, in his case by arguing individual commands set out the implications of the Decalogue.[23]

Such attempts to discern an underlying logic to the Levitical laws are inevitably speculative. Conservative scholars have necessarily spent considerable time refuting more progressive readings, leading to a general concern that the exact context of these laws is hard to establish, any underlying logic is unclear and hard to definitively prove, and the extent to which they can straightfowardly be applied to modern questions is therefore uncertain. The overall effect of this has been to downplay these passages in discussion of the biblical texts. Stott, for example, consistently argues against Bailey's dismissal of the texts, but until his 4th edition, where he cites Webb (2001) to argue that the laws indicate a concern for boundaries established in creation, he drew little from them. Ultimately these texts form a very minor part of his argument that centres on an interpretation of Genesis 2.

As in other areas, the more recent work of Gagnon (2001) and Davidson (2007) has challenged this consensus that the Levitical law is less relevant. They both advance the argument that the fact that the Levitical prohibitions are for offences described as *toevah* 'abomination', means they should be understood to be offences against a foundational creation order – homosexual acts violate the created integrity of male and female.[24] They are not so much immoral actions as denial of a fundamental truth of creation. For Gagnon, this understanding ties the commandments in Leviticus closely to Genesis 1 and 2 as central texts for approaching modern questions of human sexuality. It is Gagnon's argument that is presented by Paul (2014) as the 'traditionalist' reading of the passages (despite the fact that they derive from twenty-first-century scholarship). Similarly, Webb (2001) argues that the Levitical laws highlight sexual boundaries that prohibit immoral mixing of gender distinctives, and that these boundaries are 'transcultural', rooted in creation, and therefore still relevant. In fact, he argues on this basis that it is illegitimate for non-complementarian evangelicals to argue that there are no created differences between men and women.[25]

In conclusion, although pre-modern discussion accepted the Levitical prohibitions of same-sex activity on face value, modern critical scholarship beginning with Bailey has thrown doubt on their relevance. The context, intent and applicability to modern life of Old Testament law has been a significant area of critical debate in modern Old Testament scholarship, and arguing for the direct applicability of these prohibitions to modern sexual ethics has therefore been highly contested. Some of the modern critical questions have even been disseminated among non-academic audiences via popular liberal writing (so that evangelicals arguing for a direct application of Levitical texts are likely to be asked how they feel about shellfish and mixed fabrics). The difficulties this has posed for 'naive' readings of the Levitical texts has resulted in a downplaying of these texts in modern evangelical approaches, some of which (Stott 1984, 1990) have acknowledged there are reasons to be doubtful of how these texts should be applied. Despite this, there has always been a tradition of modern evangelical scholarship that has argued for the continued relevance of these texts, which has been much bolstered by considerable recent scholarly work in this area by Gagnon (2001) and Davidson (2007).

Pauline vice lists: 1 Corinthians 6.9–10; 1 Timothy 1.9–10

Both of these letters contain 'vice lists', conventionalized lists of well-known sins which the author exhorts the reader to distance themselves from. There is a good deal of similarity between the two lists, and in particular they both contain terms that have generally been understood to refer to male homosexual offenders. No explanation is provided for the inclusion of any of the vices, creating the impression that it was expected that the reasons for their inclusion would be self-evident. These texts were read straightfowardly in pre-modern tradition as condemning men engaging in same-sex acts as not worthy of inclusion in the kingdom, though they tended not to be frequently referenced in relation to teaching on sexuality. The emphasis by Roberts (2022) on reading these texts as specifically singling out same-sex offences above others as ones that exclude people from the kingdom, and therefore as constituting first order issues of obedience is not shared by most interpreters, ancient or modern, who recognize this as a conventional list of representative sins, not a singling out of a special category of first order sins.[26] Gagnon is representative of modern evangelical interpreters in connecting the list of offences here to the Decalogue, the implication being not that these are especially heinous offences, but that they stand for a life lived outside the values of the kingdom in the broadest sense.[27]

Although there is no term in Greek that entirely corresponds to the modern idea of a sexually active gay person, pre-modern tradition had little doubt that the key terms *malakoi* and *arsenokoitai* were meant to be read as referencing men engaging in same sex acts. *Malakoi* in particular is a term used in Greek literature to describe effeminate men. *Arsenokoitai* is not a term used in wider classical literature, but pre-modern scholars had little doubt what it applied to. Calvin unhesitatingly references 'that monstrous pollution which was but too prevalent in Greece' in his commentary.[28] The authorized version had interpreted the terms as 'effeminate' and 'abusers of themselves with mankind'. Modern translations revealed a range of understandings. The original RSV (1946, 1952) had rendered both words as 'homosexuals', a translation later taken up by the NASB (1966) which Bailey strongly criticized for failing to distinguish between orientation and practice. The 1973 revision of the RSV changed this to 'sexual perverts', with the NRSV (1989) then changing this to 'male prostitutes' and 'sodomites', restoring the reference to two terms, but inserting a reference to Genesis 19 that does not appear in the text.

Bailey's preferred translation referred to the two as passive and active partners in gay sex, which likely meant they were referring to specific sexual practices of the day and could not be directly applied to modern debate, an interpretation supported by Moffatt, whose rendering of the terms as 'catamite' and 'sodomite' was taken up by the Jerusalem Bible (1966). Stott (1984) supported Bailey's translation and critique of the original RSV translation, but was silent on the issues of direct application to modern debate.[29] Early evangelical interpreters tended to see the texts as clearly referring to those engaging in same-sex behaviour, but saw the passages as fairly marginal compared to the fuller treatment in Romans 1. Few followed Stott in highlighting the difficulty of English translations as 'homosexuals', and Lovelace (1978) comfortably quoted from the NASB text as 'homosexuals', arguing that Christians are called to repent and reorient themselves.[30] More progressive evangelicals, such as Mollenkott and Scanzoni (1978) began to actively raise concerns about the translation of the two terms – if they were referring to very specific same-sex practices that were pederastic or exploitative then there was every reason to think that they could not be straightforwardly applied to the modern debate, where no one was arguing for acceptance of either of these practices.[31]

Evangelical interpretation of these passages was transformed by the argument of Wright (1984) that *arsenokoitai* was a word either invented by Paul or another Hellenistic Jewish writer based on the Septuagint version of Leviticus 18.22 and 20.3, meaning that it has the same general reference to male same-sex acts as the Levitical law.[32] The argument has gained critical support over time and is now broadly accepted. This bolstered evangelical tendencies to interpret these passages as minor but supporting passages that should be understood to demonstrate a connection between Paul's sexual ethics and the sexual ethics of the Levitical laws, demonstrating a consistently negative evaluation of homosexual acts throughout scripture. Notably, however, even among conservatives there is not agreement that we can be sure the terms used apply universally to all forms of homosexual behaviour.[33]

In conclusion, the Pauline vice lists have never been central to biblical understandings of sexuality, but pre-modern tradition always understood them as referring to same-sex acts. Modern critical study has raised questions around the translation of the key terms which led some to assert that they could not be directly applied to the modern debate. However, the work of Wright (1984) has been significant in supporting a reading of these passages that sees them as directly drawing on Levitical law and therefore having broad application.

Romans 1

Next to Genesis 19, Romans 1 was the text that had held most significance for pre-modern Christian tradition on sexuality. As he begins his explanation of the gospel he is preaching, Paul sets out the way in which both Jews and gentiles come under God's judgement. His brief sketch of the way in which gentile society has turned away from the truth highlights its idolatry, but also prominently features male and female homosexual desire and behaviour as exemplifying their disobedience. Paul's use of the term 'against nature' to describe homosexual desire had been profoundly influential, with the term 'unnatural vice' or 'the sin against nature' vying with 'sodomy' as the most common way of describing homosexual offences in church law. Aquinas made this connection in his commentary on Romans, arguing that:

> Something is said to be against the nature of the human being by reason of the genus, which is 'animal'. Now it is manifest that, according to the intention of nature, the intercourse of the sexes in animals is ordered to the act of generation, whence all manners of intercourse, from which generation cannot follow, are against the nature of the human being.[34]

This interpretation of Romans 1, although it owed more to philosophy than a close reading of the text, cemented the idea that 'the sin against nature' was a sin against the created order, which made it very different from 'natural' sins like fornication and adultery. Aquinas' interpretation of 'the sin against nature' as being the penalty for idolatry was more clearly derived from the biblical text, though for Aquinas this was understood to link it closely to Genesis 19:

> It seems to have begun at the same time as idolatry, namely in the time of Abraham, when idolatry is believed to have begun. For that reason and at that time it is first read of as having been punished among the Sodomites.

This pre-modern interpretation of 'against nature' to mean 'not directed towards procreation' and the understanding that homosexual sin was equivalent to idolatry and therefore represented the most serious form of sexual sin had significant influence on pre-modern tradition, as we noted in Chapter 1.

Bailey's interpretation of Romans 1 was that, like the Leviticus passages, it was a piece of rhetorical condemnation of pagans that sought to emphasize their sinfulness by reference to some offences commonly emphasized in Hellenistic Jewish critique of Gentile culture. Paul could be confident his readers would recognize homosexual offence as conventionally repellent. Because of its largely rhetorical purpose, and the fact that the sins being referred to were ones already known to be particularly abhorrent, Bailey argued that the passage added little new to an understanding of sexuality. It was simply drawing on an earlier pre-Christian tradition to illustrate a point rather than developing it in any particularly distinctive way. In addition, he argued that the (highly unusual) reference to female homosexuality was so obscure that it might not even be a reference to female same-sex acts at all, but to other female sex acts that would be considered to run counter to the accepted norm by devout Jews. On this basis, he argued the entire passage had no relevance to modern debate.[35]

Bailey's evaluation has been rejected by a majority of scholars, who have consistently identified Romans 1 as a highly significant passage for understanding the theological framework within which biblical teaching on sexuality is set, and have particularly drawn attention to the way in which the passage sets an understanding of sexuality in the context of creation, with homosexuality being seen as against God's intention in creation. This point was brought out in the earliest evangelical writings on the subject in Field (1976), Lovelace (1978), Atkinson (1979), in Cranfield's influential commentary on Romans (1975), and was even supported by the Church of England Report *Homosexual Relationships* (1979), (which although seeing the biblical material as inconclusive highlighted the link to the order of creation in Romans 1 as significant in a way Bailey had not).[36] However, *Homosexual Relationships* suggested that being rooted in a creation order did not necessarily mean that something was immutable and capable of finding fulfilment in only one way, a conclusion that most evangelical interpreters have resisted. By and large, conservative evangelical commentators have assumed almost without argument that if a biblical text links something to the created order this gives it an enduring significance (it communicates a transcultural truth in Webb's terms). Thus Stott was able to draw on Cranfield to support the understanding that 'against nature' meant 'contrary to the intention of the creator', and therefore held ultimate authority without needing to follow Aquinas in linking it to the creator's command to procreate.[37]

Conservative evangelical discussion of Romans 1 has tended to be largely focused on defending its significance against progressive arguments that Paul's discussion of men turning away from women and being given over to desire for each other represents a time-bound perspective that is incompatible with either modern understandings of orientation or modern same-sex relationships and is therefore irrelevant to modern debate. This was the argument presented by Mollenkott and Scanzoni (1978) among others. We have already noted in Chapter 1 that many early evangelical writers such as Atkinson (1979) and Stott (1984) readily acknowledged that ancient writers like Paul did not have a modern understanding of orientation. This did not prevent them from also systematically arguing that this cannot be used to rule out the relevance of a passage concerned with behaviour that violates created order.[38] This willingness to acknowledge that there is a genuine gap between modern and ancient understandings of sexuality began to be set aside with Schmidt (1995), who argued that although Paul would not have thought in modern terms about orientation, his willingness to view male and female same-sex desire as fundamentally the same phenomena was a unique perspective in the modern world and one far closer to modern understandings of 'homosexuality'. For this reason Paul could be assumed to be able to step out of the conventional understandings of his age. This point was supported by Bonnington and Fyall in 1996.[39] Gagnon (2001) went further, engaging in a considerable survey of intertestamental and classical literature to argue that Paul was *not* a unique voice in recognizing male and female homosexuality as the same sort of offence, but that there was evidence of this understanding in the ancient world. This meant that there was a close enough understanding of the existence of something akin to modern conceptions of homosexuality in the ancient world that Paul can be assumed to have been aware of the possibility of unchosen same-sex desire leading to stable loving relationships akin to marriage, a position that would not be supported by most classical scholars.[40]

Although evangelical scholars have always seen Romans 1 as the most significant of the texts that directly relate to homosexuality there has been a tendency within the tradition of interpretation behind the consensus position to see all of these texts as less significant than Genesis 1 and 2. The roots of this approach can be seen in Atkinson (1979), but it is given its decisive formation in Stott (1984). Stott contrasts the negative teaching of the texts that directly address homosexuality with the positive teaching of the church about opposite sex marriage, which derives from Genesis 1 and 2 and its notion of 'one flesh union' between man and woman. On this basis, Stott effectively treats all the texts that directly address homosexuality, including Romans 1, as marginal to his central argument, relativizing any interpretational issues. All these texts are called upon to demonstrate is that scripture is consistently negative in its evaluation of homosexuality.

In conclusion, unlike Genesis 19, Romans 1 has remained a text that is widely regarded as the one of the most significant of the texts directly addressing homosexuality. The theological evaluation of homosexual desire as 'against nature', understood as violating a divine order in creation, remains key. However, evangelicals have moved away from a traditional understanding that this refers to non-procreative acts to an understanding that this refers to acts undermining gender distinctiveness. A certain synergy between interpretations of the Levitical law and Romans 1 is apparent here in the analysis offered by Gagnon and Davidson, with both passages seen as highlighting homosexual offence as particularly symbolic of rejection of divine order in creation. However, there has been a consistent tendency to follow Stott's (1984) preference to stress the positive teaching on marriage, rather than the negative teaching on homosexuality, as the core of an evangelical interpretation of scripture. This has the effect of relativizing the significance of all interpretational questions around the texts directly addressing sexuality.

Some provisional conclusions

We have surveyed the history of interpretation of all the biblical texts that directly reference homosexuality, with particular attention to how modern evangelicals have interpreted them. It is clear that modern evangelicals do not interpret these texts in the same way that pre-modern Christian tradition did, and indeed much of the homophobic pre-modern interpretation of these texts is repudiated by modern evangelicals. Modern evangelical interpretation therefore represents a substantially new and critically informed approach to these texts. It is also clear that modern evangelical tradition represents a research active field that is constantly being shaped and challenged by new work being undertaken by scholars.

There is no single settled pattern of interpretation of any of these individual texts that is universally recognized as 'correct' by modern evangelicals. Conservative evangelical scholars continue to interpret individual texts in different ways (for example Hays and Gagnon's disagreement over the relevance of Genesis 19) while continuing to recognize each other as supporting the consensus position. On the whole, conservative evangelicals are willing to tolerate diversity within their own ranks on the relevance and interpretation of the texts that directly address homosexuality as long as a broad consensus is maintained that all of these texts are negative in their evaluation of homosexual activity. This is because within the consensus position, following Stott, all of these texts are viewed as representing the negative teaching of the church. Their function within the argument is simply to prove that the church has never condoned same-sex activity. The weight of the biblical interpretation advanced by the consensus position actually falls not on these texts but on Genesis 1 and 2, the texts presented as the positive teaching of the church. We will therefore now turn to considering this core aspect of modern evangelical biblical interpretation.

The significance of heterosexual marriage in creation: Genesis 1 and 2

In 2022, the Church of England Evangelical Council (CEEC) released a series of shorter follow-up videos to its *Beautiful Story* video. One of these, entitled *How important are our differences?* explicitly addressed the question of whether sexuality constituted a first order issue.[41] While acknowledging that there are certain areas where disagreement between Christians is allowed, Santosh Thomas states that disagreement on sexuality is not possible because Jesus says these are issues of eternal significance: 'His teaching tells us this is a matter of primary importance.'

You may have noticed that we have just surveyed all of the biblical texts that are agreed by scholars to directly address homosexuality and none of them featured teaching by Jesus, so this insistence that disagreement on sexuality means turning away from the direct teaching of Jesus might seem rather mystifying. However, the video helpfully ends with a biblical text displayed on screen so that it is clear what teaching of Jesus is being referred to here. The text shown is Matthew 19.4–5: 'Haven't you read that at the beginning the creator made them male and female and said for this reason a man will leave his father and mother and be united with his wife and the two will become one flesh?'

Matthew 19.4–5 is part of Jesus' answer to a tricky question on divorce law posed by some Pharisees, where he quotes directly from Genesis 1.27 and 2.24. The unquoted verse 6 is Jesus' commentary on the texts, showing that the central detail Jesus is drawing from Genesis 1 and 2 is that God's intention in creation was that marriage should be the creation of 'one flesh' and therefore permanent, thus answering the question he had been posed about the legitimacy of divorce.

You might be forgiven at this point for continuing to be rather mystified as to why the video assumes Matthew 19.4–5 might be assumed to indicate an area where the early church was very clear what Jesus taught on sexuality. After all, he says nothing about homosexuality, and even on divorce Jesus appears elsewhere to suggest that adultery might constitute valid grounds for divorce. However, this is one of the areas where it is clear that the CEEC output is intended for an internal evangelical audience who are already very familiar with the broad position being stated. Matthew 19.4–5 and the parallel passage in Mark 10.4–9 have a prominent role in Stott's (1984) discussion of sexuality. These verses are presented by Stott as Jesus' teaching on marriage: a permanent public union between one man and one woman that is consumated in sexual union. On this basis he argues that scripture envisages no other context in which sexual intercourse is permitted. (It is notable that, in line with his other attempts to distance a modern evangelical ethic from earlier homophobic tradition, this allows Stott to hold up a single ideal from which any departure is equally blameworthy – arguing contra Aquinas that on this basis same-sex sexual relationships are not a worse sin than any other). The CEEC video is therefore asserting that Jesus' brief reference to Genesis 1 and 2 in Matthew 19.4–5 should be heard as implying the authority of Christ lies behind the whole theology of marriage and sexuality that Stott has derived from them.

It is important to recognize the way that these texts are linked in conservative evangelical thought, as it explains how a theology on sexuality never explicitly stated by Jesus is regarded as being his teaching, and how a set of New Testament texts and concerns are regarded as the interpretative key to Old Testament texts that do not explicitly state a theology of sexuality. Having established the relevance of Genesis 1 and 2 to questions of sexual ethics by reference to Matthew 19, Stott suggests that the creation narratives present man and woman being created equal yet with complementary sexual natures, designed to be each other's sexual partners:

> Heterosexual intercourse in marriage is more than a union; it is a kind of reunion ... It is not a union of alien persons who do not belong to one another and cannot appropriately become one flesh ... much more than a union of bodies; it is a blending of complementary personalities through which, in the midst of prevailing alienation, the rich created oneness of human being is experienced again.[42]

Stott engages in further exploration of this theme in his chapter on male and female equality, advocating a complementarian understanding that sees male headship as part of the created difference between men and women. A theological understanding of gendered humanity that is rooted in this particular interpretation of the creation narratives therefore underpins not only evangelical approaches to same-sex relationships, but also divorce and remarriage and male-female equality.

The basic groundwork offered by Stott was much reinforced by Gagnon (2001), who offers a detailed reading of Genesis 1 and 2. For Gagnon male-female complementarity expressed in a one-flesh union is integral to God's purposes for humanity as created in his image, going far beyond the need for procreation:

God's intent for human sexuality is imbedded in the material creation of gendered beings ... 'Male and female he created them' probably intimates that the fullness of God's 'image' comes together in the union of male and female in marriage (and not, one could infer, from same-sex unions).[43]

He argues that the Genesis 2 account downplays an emphasis on procreation in favour of an emphasis on a complementarian relationship that proclaims the divine order. Gagnon's argument is that this forms a strand of tradition throughout scripture, expressed in Levitical law and Paul's discussion in Romans that sees male-female one-flesh union as God's intention in creation, and regards departure from this as abhorrent. Gagnon argues therefore that Jesus' choice to use 'one-flesh' language in Matthew 19 should be understood as a conscious alignment with this deep theme in scripture that affirms the necessity of male-female sexual compatibility in marriage. The work of Gagnon has been further supported by the substantial work of Davidson (2007) in his magisterial survey of sexuality in the entirety of the Old Testament. Both stress the sense of an irreducible difference and non-interchangeability between men and women as central to the created order.

It is important at this point to recognize two things about this developed tradition of reading Genesis 1 and 2. The first is that this is a very modern and recent tradition, as Davidson acknowledges.[44] In many ways it builds on the mid-twentieth-century work of Barth, who advanced a detailed interpretation of the gendered creation of man as male and female as a revelation of God's nature and desire for reunion with humanity, and as the crown of creation: 'God's whole intercourse with man will now be strictly related to man conjoined as male and female ... Only as ordered by God at creation can this encounter be normal and good in its relationship to God. Any other form of the relationship between man and woman alters their mutual relationship to God.'[45] Barth's central focus here is an understanding of the male-female relationship, but the implications for sexuality are obvious. The one flesh understanding may also be influenced by von Rad's work on Genesis, but either way it is a very specifically twentieth-century tradition of interpretation of the creation narratives.⁴⁶ As we shall see it is very different from pre-modern biblical interpretation of the creation narratives.

The second point to recognize is that this tradition of evangelical interpretation has strong links to a complementarian understanding of masculine and feminine nature – which is a central rather than incidental aspect of this tradition. We have already noted that this is a central implication for Barth (though evangelical complementarians take issue with the detail of his exegesis). It is important to recognize, however, that Stott advances the exact same interpretation of the exact same passages elsewhere in *Issues* to support a view of gender relations that sees male headship in marriage and church as the divinely ordained pattern of creation: 'what creation has established, no culture is able to destroy ... headship itself is creational, not cultural'.⁴⁷ The idea that the creation narratives set out a divinely instituted pattern of marriage that is rooted in the necessary difference and non-interchangeability between the genders is central to evangelical complementarian argument:

> At its very heart, marriage is not a human custom, variable according to changing times; it is a divinely created institution, defined for all ages and all cultures in our shared, primeval, perfect existence ... God did not create man and woman in an undifferentiated way, and their mere maleness and femaleness identify their respective roles.⁴⁸

Precisely for this reason, this interpretation of the creation narratives is resisted by many evangelical scholars who wish to promote a more egalitarian understanding, and point to procreation as the *only* implication of the 'one flesh' language.⁴⁹

My point here is not to make a case that either interpretation is correct, but rather to point out that evangelicals commonly suggest male headship, unlike sexuality, is a second order issue on which disagreement can be accepted. The implied argument of the CEEC video (drawing on Stott and Gagnon) is that sexuality is a first order issue because it is based in the doctrinal principle of the complementarity of male-female nature that is clear in the creation narratives and reinforced by Jesus' reference to it in the gospels. The centrality of this interpretation to both a position on sexuality and on women's ministry makes that distinction hard to maintain. Either faithfulness to the clear teaching of scripture in Genesis 1 and 2 (as implying the complementarity and non-interchangeability of genders) is a first order issue or it isn't. Webb's work seems to be prompted by this realization. His *Slaves, Women and Homosexuals* (2001) is a conservative attempt to establish the legitimacy of conservative disagreement over complementarity by establishing that a progressive reading of scripture can be regarded as legitimate (as in the case of slavery) without having to open the door to progressive readings conservatives assume are clearly illegitimate (as in the case of homosexuality). He does this by shifting the emphasis away from the overriding importance of the creation narratives and back towards the overwhelming negativity of the texts directly addressing homosexuality. This is in some ways a tacit admission that rooting the 'clear teaching of scripture' in the creation narratives alone raises these sorts of questions.

Teaching on Christian marriage and 'one flesh' union in the early church

I have already noted that the early church did not tend to interpret Genesis 1 and 2 in the way modern evangelicals do, did not hold to the same understanding of the positive place of sexuality in marriage, and tended to see procreation rather than complementary relationship between the genders as the primary purpose of sexual relationship. The 'positive tradition of Christian marriage' that is presented by modern evangelicals is therefore in fact a profoundly modern creation that is decisively different from earlier pre-modern Christian understandings.

In fact, Genesis 1 and 2 were only rarely referenced in pre-modern discussion of same sex acts. Even when (as we have seen in Aquinas' discussion of Romans 1), a theologian makes a reference to the way homosexuality goes against the created nature of human beings, this tended not to involve discussion of the creation narratives, but to philosophical presuppositions about nature. The most prominent example of the 'one flesh' language being used in pre-modern tradition to interpret same sex acts is in Chrysostum's notoriously homophobic *Homily IV* on Romans 1, where he describes homosexuality or 'the mad lust after males' as the vilest of affections, which it is impossible to truly derive pleasure from, that is by nature a diabolical inversion of the order of creation as a whole:

> Name what sin you will, none will equal this lawlessness ... thou hast not made thyself a dog out of a man, but an animal more disgraceful than this ... it is not the same thing to have changed into a woman as to continue a man and yet have become a woman, or rather neither this nor that ... How many hells shall be enough for such? But if thou scoffest at hell and believest not that fire, remember Sodom!... Consider how great is that sin to have forced hell to appear before its time![50]

In Chrysostum's discussion of sexuality the 'one flesh' language of the creation narratives is appealed to in order to interpret the theological significance of God giving the gentiles over to homosexual desire. Chrysostum *does* seem to see a necessary created sexual complementarity of male and female in a similar way to modern evangelical complementarians (mentioning the respective roles of man as instructor of the woman and woman as helper of the man), but it isn't abandonment of these roles in a relationship that he sees as the principal evil of same sex activity. Abandonment of created gender roles is referenced as evidence of what has happened rather than the reason why it is problematic. To provide a theological explanation for the enormity of homosexual sin, Chrysostum uses the 'one flesh' language to highlight God's intention in creation that all humanity be united, arguing that the truly diabolical nature of homosexual desire is found in the fact that it leads to disunity:

For 'the twain', it says, 'shall be one flesh.' But this the desire of intercourse effected, and united the sexes to one another. The desire the devil having taken away, and having turned the course thereof into another fashion, he thus sundered the sexes from one another, and made the one to become two in opposition to the law of God.[51]

Chrysostum here uses the 'one flesh' language to interpret homosexual desire as linked not only to rebellion against God and abandonment of our created roles, but even more so to destruction, enmity, sedition and war. The significance of man and woman being 'one flesh' is therefore not that they are created to be distinctly different, but that they are created to be the same.

In understanding pre-modern Christian tradition around Genesis 1 and 2 it is important to recognize that by and large it did not tend to emphasize a necessary created complementary difference between men and women. In fact, the reverse is more nearly true. The early church fathers (most of whom were celibate monks) operated in a tradition in which celibacy rather than marriage was understood to be the highest Christian calling, and one that was open to both men and women. A holy female celibate could be seen as someone who had transcended the limitations of her gender, and could be revered as a teacher, as Gregory of Nyssa described his older sister Macrina.[52] Unlike in a Christian tradition like modern evangelicalism, where (as frankly acknowledged in *The Beautiful Story*) the normal, aspirational, and most celebrated pattern of life is marriage, the early church revered the celibate life. They shared an understanding, following the teaching of Christ and Paul, that in the kingdom of heaven people will not marry but be like the angels, and that Christ had done away with division between male and female. Maximus the Confessor, writing of the achievement of Christ stated:

> I think, that there was perhaps another way, foreknown to God, for human beings to increase, if the first human being

had kept the commandment ... Thus God-made-man has done away with the difference and division of nature into male and female, which human nature in no way needed for generation, as some hold, and without which it would perhaps have been possible.[53]

Far from the possibility of sexual union being God's perfect intention in creation then, the early church fathers tended to assume that sexuality and sexual desire was a result of the Fall, and sexual differentiation itself would be removed when we are made perfect. Gregory of Nyssa argued:

> The grace we look for is a certain return to the first life, bringing back again to paradise those who were cast out from it. If then the life of those restored is closely related to that of the angels, it is clear that the life before the transgression was a kind of angelic life.[54]

As the Christian disciple grew in sanctity of life, these differences of male and female, never really part of God's intent, would fall away. The only early church father to really challenge the idea that sexuality was a result of the Fall rather than God's intention in creation was Augustine, who argued in *On the literal interpretation of Genesis* that sexual differentiation was a good part of God's intention in creation, but he argued this solely on the grounds that it was necessary in order to produce children.

The early church tended to interpret the 'one-flesh' language of Genesis 2.24 as a foreshadowing of the union between Christ and the church, rather than communicating a theological truth about the necessary sexual complementarity of men and women. This is the sense in which it was used by John Chrysostum in his interpretation of Romans 1. For the early church, the theological significance of Genesis 2.24 was therefore the fact that it pointed to the ultimate unity of all humanity in Christ, in whom all division (including sexual division) would be removed, not that it highlighted the necessary theological significance of the sexual difference between man and woman as God's perfect intention in creation.

In fact the early church, like much of its surrounding patriarchal culture, tended not to naturally see men and women as complementary partners at all. The prevailing pre-modern view of the sexes was closer to the idea that women were a form of defective man than it was to the idea that men and women were equal but different with strengths that complemented each other. This alone would have rendered modern evangelical exegesis of Genesis 1 and 2 incomprehensible to them. Augustine, in the midst of setting out his radical case that sexuality for the purpose of producing children was part of God's good intention in creation, argues in passing that procreation is the *only* possible explanation for God creating a woman as a helper for Adam:

> Now suppose the woman was not made for the man to be his helper in begetting children, then how would she be able to help him? ... [Not for physical labour, because] a male helper would be better, and the same could be said of the comfort of another's presence ... How much more agreeably could two male friends, rather than a man and a woman, enjoy companionship and conversation in a life together ... Consequently I do not see in what sense the woman was made as a helper for the man if not for the sake of bearing children.[55]

If God's intention had simply been to provide a companion in labour, a friend in solitude, and a partner in conversation in a shared life (in other words if God's intent had been to provide the sort of relational complementarity modern evangelicals argue only a male-female relationship can provide) then Augustine argues that God would simply have created another man.

The degree to which procreation rather than companionship was seen as the central purpose of marriage in the pre-modern church cannot be overestimated. As modern people, used to sex being a normal and expected part of marriage but having children being a choice, we naturally view marriage very differently. Although Augustine's writings on marriage made a case for the acceptance of marriage as a way of life that was recognized as being as high a spiritual calling as celibacy, having the dignity of a sacrament, the sense that marriage was a second best calling persisted due to the emphasis on clerical celibacy in the West. Renunciation of sex was recognized as an act of devotion, practised by the most religious. In the medieval church, an influential strand of teaching held that married people were understood to sin if they had sex with each other purely for enjoyment rather than for the purpose of procreation. This only changed at the beginning of the modern era with Protestants writing against Catholic teaching on celibacy. Luther argued strongly that marriage was God's intention for all who were not given the gift of celibacy, that monks and nuns should leave their monasteries and get married, and that sexuality was God-given, so that men and women should fulfil God's purpose and not deny their natural urges by marrying.[56] He saw marriage, sex and children as a full part of God's intention in creation, encouraging husbands and wives to delight in each other, laying some of the foundations for the modern evangelical understanding of Christian marriage. It is vital to realize that evangelical teaching on sex and marriage represents a modern revision of Christian tradition, based on a critical rereading of biblical texts that, for example, allows Song of Songs to be read literally as a celebration of sexuality rather than allegorically as entirely concerned with the relationship between Christ and the church. This is the sort of sex-positive biblical vision that is set out in Harrison's *A Better Story*:

> Our sexual attractions and desires – our embodied experience – show us the passionate nature of God's love ... Our 'pit-of-the-stomach' experience of desire, including the erotic tones of attraction and arousal, bear witness to, and direct us towards, the end of all longing in Jesus Christ.[57]

It represents a profoundly modern rereading of scripture, as he himself recognizes. This doesn't mean this is not the right way to understand scripture. It means that evangelicals already implicitly accept the fact that modern critical tools have enabled biblical truths to be discerned that were not apparent to pre-modern Christian tradition.

In summary then, the modern evangelical interpretation of the 'one flesh' language of Genesis 2.24 as implying the necessary relational complementarity of men and women in marriage is distinctly modern and very different from preceding tradition. Early church tradition saw marriage as necessarily between a man and a woman very specifically because procreation was the primary purpose of marriage (even if they acknowledged that marriage could also provide companionship). This is part of a much wider modern evangelical rereading of scripture that has transformed the way sex and sexuality are understood.

Scripture as the basis for sexuality as a first order area of doctrine

The claim that adherence to the consensus position is a first order issue in regard to the interpretation of scripture takes several forms. One, already discussed above, is that there are particular passages whose meaning is so clear that failure to acknowledge this represents unfaithfulness – a proud refusal to submit to God's will. Roberts seems to regard the clear listing of homosexual offence in Pauline vice lists as such a passage. As we have explored at more length, *How important are our differences?* suggests that the creation narratives, understood as a basic biblical understanding of human nature, are another such passage. Paul's suggestion that sexuality must be seen as a first order issue because it revolves around a basic biblical anthropology is a slightly more sophisticated version of this, pointing to Gagnon's analysis of male-female difference as a key biblical truth seen in a variety of passages.[58] Gagnon's own argument seems to be that (having engaged in detail over around 300 pages with other biblical scholars in order to disprove their exegesis of the key passages to his satisfaction) the meaning of scripture can now unproblematically be asserted to be 'clear' and any remaining disputes therefore reduced to discussions of how such clear and authoritative teaching should be applied.[59] In all these cases I have shown that it is hard to maintain the idea that scripture is so clear that failure to adopt the consensus position must be understood as faithlessness when the suggested 'clear' meaning is not universally accepted even among evangelicals. In regard to the creation narratives in particular, the fact that differing evangelical interpretations of these passages are accepted in relation to women's ministry make it hard to argue that they cannot be in regard to sexuality. Without agreement that the creation narratives clearly teach gender distinctiveness and non-interchangeability, Gagnon's wider argument that this is the biblical theme that lies behind the negative evaluation of homosexuality in all other texts loses much of its interpretative power.

A second and more sophisticated form that the claim takes is that there is a consistent thread of meaning that can be discerned in a variety of passages (but is not entirely dependent on any specific interpretation of any one of them) and that this constitutes a doctrinal truth of scripture, departure from which is unfaithfulness in the same way as denial of creedal truth. Oliver O'Donovan's careful analysis of the sexuality debate is helpful here, in noting that a dispute over doctrinal truth must consist in much more than moral disagreement. If, for example, two people were to agree that homosexual acts were not God's intention in creation but were to propose different pastoral responses to this, one for example arguing that this should be pastorally accommodated by an acceptance of same-sex relationships within a fallen world and the other disagreeing, then this does not constitute a doctrinal disagreement. Doctrinal disagreement arises when two people propose a different ethical response based on a fundamentally different interpretation of the truth of the world we live in.[60] This can legitimately be regarded as a first order issue if the truth concerned can genuinely be shown to be central to historic Christian faith. As noted above, this understanding of sexuality as a first order issue of obedience to scripture is not dependent on agreeing to a certain interpretation of any individual passage. It would be true whether Stott's interpretation of Genesis 1 and 2 was accepted or not.

It is important to recognize that most popular presentations of a conservative position do not take the degree of care O'Donovan does in articulating exactly what is at issue, often suggesting that the issue is simple adherence to traditional sexual ethics (ignoring the distinction he makes between different moral choices and ethical disagreement).[61] However, proposing to accept same-sex marriage as equivalent to opposite sex marriage and therefore both as being equally God's good gift to humanity might be a first order issue, if it could plausibly be argued that this represents adopting a fundamentally different doctrinal understanding of marriage rather than a different pastoral outworking of the same doctrinal understanding. For O'Donovan himself, as is clear from the St Andrew's Day statement that he was a signatory to, the recognition of heterosexual marriage and singleness as the only two appropriate patterns of Christian life set out in scripture and tradition can be regarded as having such doctrinal status.[62] Not only does this represent a clear thread of meaning in scripture, it is one that has always been recognized in Christian tradition despite not featuring in the creeds.

Although this approach to regarding sexuality as a first order issue is not dependent on set interpretations of any particular passages (indeed cannot be, as part of its argument is that it represents a continuity of a tradition still held to by Christians who interpreted all these passages differently) it does have to face a different challenge. As is clear from the above discussion, much of what is now presented by conservatives as integral to a Christian doctrine of marriage has a relatively recent origin. The shift of emphasis from procreation to male-female complementarity as central to the purpose of marriage has been a modern one that has become cemented through the advent of reliable contraception and male-female equality, even if the ideal of companionship in marriage has never been entirely absent. Sexuality as a good gift of God rather than a result of the Fall is a relatively modern theological idea, even if its origins can be traced back to Augustine. Consent has come to be seen as of vital importance in modern marriage in a way that would be alien to those where arranged marriages were common. In scripture itself there seems to be a clear sense of development from acceptance of polygamy to monogamy as the ideal. Although there is good reason to recognize the modern evangelical doctrine of marriage as a faithful development of ancient tradition it *is* a development, not a simple continuation. Marriage does not mean the same thing today as it did two thousand years ago even within the church.

Once it is realized that current conservative understandings of marriage represent a modern development of tradition it becomes clear that the sexuality debate can be understood as a debate over *the extent to which* the tradition can legitimately be developed, not as a debate over whether we should see an unchanging scriptural tradition as having authority. Where conservatives have developed the tradition towards emphasizing the relational aspect of marriage over the procreational, yet kept a strong sense of the importance of sexual difference, progressives wish to go further in de-emphasizing the importance of sexual difference within marriage. Disagreement over the legitimacy of such a move clearly falls in O'Donovan's terms into the area of doctrinal difference. However, recognition that the significance of the disagreement is potentially of the first order should not mean ruling out the possibility that just as conservatives have already accommodated development of the doctrine of Christian marriage and advanced new interpretation of scripture to support it, further development may also be legitimate. O'Donovan's call to recognize the possibility that this is a first order area of disagreement is therefore not an attempt to prevent debate, but a call for careful discernment by the whole church that should not be pre-empted by attempts to denounce the 'other side' as beyond the pale.

Conclusion

This survey of twentieth and twenty-first-century evangelical interpretation of scripture is by nature partial. There are in most cases more issues of interpretation (and a wider variety of suggested interpretations) in regard to all of these passages than those I have highlighted – I have simply discussed some of the more significant areas. My intention throughout has not been to give a comprehensive overview of evangelical understanding, but to highlight the fact that despite popular-level rhetoric that this is a straightfoward issue of submission to the authority of scripture on a question where scripture is transparently clear this is far from the case. Even conservative evangelicals do not agree with each other on the 'clear meaning' of some of the key passages. The fact that some evangelicals are arguing that sexuality is a first order issue on which scripture is entirely clear *on entirely different grounds that don't relate to any of the passages I have discussed* underlines the fact that there is no agreement even among evangelicals on what the key passages are and how they should be interpreted.[63]

My point is not to suggest that conservative evangelicals are being anything other than sincere in expressing their view that they believe sexuality to be a key battleground for gospel faithfulness. My argument is simply that none of the ways the sexuality debate is popularly presented by either conservatives or progressives actually represent the complexity of what is going on in evangelical interpretation of scripture. Evangelicals are far from biblical literalists or homophobic bigots blindly parroting an unexamined tradition. Twentieth-century evangelical biblical interpretation of sexuality represents serious engagement with critical scholarship, respectfully encompasses different interpretations of complex passages, and upholds a doctrine of marriage that is thoroughly modern and radically different from pre-modern understandings. Neither progressive accusations of unreconstructed fundamentalism nor conservative protestations that they are simply setting out the plain truth of scripture can therefore be taken at face value. Most of the key insights underlying evangelical understandings are reliant on scholarship that was carried out well within living memory – in some cases within the last 20 to 30 years. There is little to suggest that interpretation of key passages will not continue to develop as new scholarship is carried out. Very clearly this is modern biblical scholarship addressing modern questions. Exploring why this obvious truth is not widely acknowledged either by conservatives or progressives will be the central focus of the next two chapters. It's a question that takes us to the heart of why the sexuality debate has become so hard to resolve, and why it is so poorly understood even by those caught up within it.

Notes

1 Roberts, Vaughan, 2022, *Together in Love and Faith? Should the Church Bless Same-Sex partnerships? – A response to the Bishop of Oxford*, https://2713aced-d665-4866-bcd0-8f7d81f2f5fe.usrfiles.com/ugd/2713ac_4f9a3958db324778b807e9507fb7c1b3.pdf, p. 25 (accessed 13.2.2023).

2 Roberts, 2022, p. 30.

3 Augustine, 1992, *Confessions* III:viii, trans. Henry Chadwick, Oxford: Oxford University Press, p. 46.

4 Third Lateran Council, edict 11, https://www.papalencyclicals.net/councils/ecum11.htm (accessed 13.2.2023).

5 Bailey, Derrick Sherwin, 1955, *Homosexuality and the Western Christian Tradition*, London: Longmans, pp. 9–28.

6 Field, David, 1976, *The Homosexual Way – A Christian Option?*, Bramcote: Grove Books, p. 10; Atkinson, David, 1979, *Homosexuals in the Christian Fellowship*, Oxford: Latimer House, pp. 79–81.

7 Church of England, 1979, *Homosexual Relationships (HR)*, p. 27; 1991, *Issues in Human Sexuality (IiHS)*, p. 10; 2003, *Some Issues in Human Sexuality (SiiHS)*, pp. 120–2.

8 Moss, Roger, 1977, *Christians and Homosexuality*, Exeter: Paternoster, p. 26; Schmidt, Thomas, 1995, *Straight and Narrow?*, Westmont, IL: InterVarsity Press, p. 87; Bonnington, Mark and Fyall, Bob, 1998, *Homosexuality and the Bible*, Cambridge: Grove Books, p. 12; Hays, Richard, 1996, *The Moral Vision of the New Testament*, Edinburgh: T&T Clark, p. 381.

9 Stott, John, 1984, *Issues Facing Christians Today*, 1st edn, Basingstoke: Marshall, Mogan & Scott, pp. 304–5; 1990, 2nd edn, p. 339–40; 1999, 3rd edn, pp. 386–8; 2006, pp. 448–51.
10 Bonnington and Fyall, 1998, p. 12, fn. 11.
11 Paul, Ian, 2014, *Same-Sex Unions*, Cambridge: Grove Books, pp. 10–11.
12 Gagnon, Robert A. J., 2001, *The Bible and Homosexual Practice*, Oxford: Abingdon, p. 71, fn. 74.
13 Davidson, Richard M., 2007, *Flame of Yahweh*, Peabody: Hendrickson, pp. 145–9.
14 Goddard, Andrew and Horrocks, Don, 2012, *Biblical and Pastoral Responses to Homosexuality*, London: Evangelical Alliance, p. 41.
15 Bailey, 1955, pp. 48–50.
16 Bailey, 1955, pp. 52–3.
17 Gagnon, 2001, pp. 100–10; Paul, 2014, p. 17; *SiiHS*, 2003, p. 126.
18 Stott, John and McCloughry, Roy, 2006, *Issues Facing Christians Today*, 2006, 4th edn, Grand Rapids, Zondervan, pp. 451–2.
19 Davidson, 2007, p. 93.
20 Bailey, 1955, p. 50.
21 Goddard and Horrocks, 2012, p. 43; Hays, 1996, p. 282.
22 Douglas, Mary, 1966, *Purity and Danger: An Analysis of Concepts of Pollution and Taboo*, London: Routledge, ch. 3; Countryman, L. William, 1988, *Dirt, Greed & Sex*, Philadelphia: Fortress, pp. 30–4.
23 Atkinson, 1979, pp. 82–6.
24 Gagnon, 2001, pp. 111–42; Davidson, 2007, pp. 149–59.
25 Webb, William J., 2001, *Slaves, Women and Homosexuals*, Westmont, IL: InterVarsity Press, p. 253.
26 Roberts, 2022, p. 41.
27 Gagnon, 2001, pp. 303–36.
28 Calvin, John, *Commentary on Corinthians*, 1573, trans. John Pringle, https://ccel.org/ccel/calvin/calcom39/calcom39.xiii.ii.html (accessed 12.2.2023).
29 Stott, 1984, pp. 307–8.
30 Lovelace, Richard F., 1978, *Homosexuality and the Church*, Thetford: Lamp Press, p. 96.
31 Mollenkett, Virginia Ramey and Scanzoni, Letha Dawson, 1978, *Is the Homosexual my Neighbour?*, New York: Harper Collins, pp. 74–8.
32 Wright, David, 'Homosexuals or Prostitutes? The meaning of arsenokoitai', *Vigiliae Christianae* 38, 1984: pp. 125–53.
33 See Webb, 2001, p. 197.
34 Aquinas, Thomas, *Commentary on Romans* 1, in Eugene Rogers ed., 2002, *Theology and Sexuality*, Oxford: Blackwell, p. 106.

35 Bailey, 1955, pp. 40–1.
36 Field, 1976, p. 11; Lovelace, 1978, pp. 91–6; Atkinson, 1979, pp. 86–90; Cranfield, C. E. B., *Commentary on Romans*, Vol. 1, Edinburgh: T&T Clark, p. 126; *HR*, 1979, pp. 31–2.
37 Stott, 1990, p. 349.
38 Atkinson, 1979, pp. 89–90, Stott, 1984, pp. 312–13.
39 Schmidt, 1995, pp. 81–3; Bonnington and Fyall, 1998, p. 21.
40 Gagnon, 2001, pp. 380–95.
41 CEEC, 2022, *How important are our differences?*, https://ceec.info/resources/gods-beautiful-story/ (accessed 13.2.2023).
42 Stott, 1984, pp. 310–11.
43 Gagnon, 2001, p. 58.
44 Davidson, 2007, pp. 17–18.
45 Barth, Karl, 1958, *Church Dogmatics*, Vol. 3/1, trans. G. W. Bromiley and T. F. Torrence, Edinburgh: T&T Clark, p. 308.
46 Von Rad, Gerhard, 1961, *Genesis*, trans. John H. Marks, London: SCM Press, p. 85.
47 Stott, 1984, p. 246.
48 Ortlund Jr., Raymond C., 'Male-female equality and male headship' in John Piper and Wayne Grudem, 2021, *Recovering Biblical Manhood and Womanhood*, Wheaton: Crossway, pp. 127–8.
49 Conway, Mary L., 'Gender in creation and fall', in Ronald W. Pierce and Cynthia Westfall eds, 2021, *Discovering Biblical Equality*, 3rd edn, London: InterVarsity Press, p. 43.
50 Chrysostom, John, 'Homily IV on Romans', in *Nicene and Post-Nicene Fathers*, Series 1, Vol. 11, ed. Philip Schaff, Edinburgh: Eerdmans, p. 358–9.
51 Chrysostom, p. 356
52 Brown, Peter, 1988, *The Body and Society*, New York: Columbia University Press, pp. 298–300.
53 Maximus the Confessor, *Book of Difficulties* 41, cited in ed. Andrew Louth, 2001, *Genesis 1–11*, Westmont, IL: InterVarsity Press, pp. 38–9.
54 Gregory of Nyssa, *On the making of man* 17, cited in ed. Louth, 2001, p. 73.
55 Augustine, *On the literal interpretation of Genesis*, cited in Louth, 2001, p. 69.
56 Thatcher, Adrian, ed., 2015, *The Oxford Handbook of Theology, Sexuality and Gender*, Oxford: Oxford University Press, p. 307.
57 Harrison, Glynn, 2016, *A Better Story: God, sex & human flourishing*, Westmont, IL: Intervarsity Press, p. 152. See his critique of tradition on p. 81.
58 Paul, 2014, p. 29.

59 Gagnon, 2001, p. 341.
60 O'Donovan, Oliver, 2009, *A Conversation Waiting to Begin*, London: SCM Press, p. 42.
61 See for example Roberts, 2022, pp. 41–2. In O'Donovan's terms, Roberts is either describing knowingly urging the acceptance of sin (which is straightfoward moral failure rather than ethical disagreement), or unknowingly doing so (which is a complex moral area, given that choosing to do something you sincerely believe to be wrong is generally also regarded as sin). In either case Roberts is not describing ethical disagreement, and therefore the question of first or second order becomes irrelevant.
62 Bradshaw, Timothy, ed., 1997, *The Way Forward?*, Cambridge: Eerdmans, p. 9.
63 Penduck, Joshua, 2022, A letter in response to the Bishop of Oxford, https://www.fulcrum-anglican.org.uk/articles/a-letter-in-response-to-the-bishop-of-oxford/ (accessed 13.2.2023).

3

Evangelicals talking to evangelicals

The Beautiful Story as a typical statement of current evangelical thinking

The previous chapters have set out some of the ways in which commonly held understandings of the sexuality debate (that it represents a conflict between traditionalists and revisionists, or between biblical literalists and free-thinking modernizers) represent misleading simplifications. It has also become apparent that even those most directly involved in the sexuality debate are not necessarily aware of its history. The fact that the evangelical consensus position represents a comparatively modern understanding that is significantly discontinuous with a profoundly homophobic Christian tradition, and the fact that evangelical and Church of England understandings of scripture only really aligned in 1991 with the publication of *Issues in Human Sexuality*, have all disappeared from the collective memory. In their place is the insistence that evangelicals are defending the received tradition of the church, and that this represents simple obedience to the clear sense of scripture. In this chapter I want to explore how the sexuality debate became so divisive.

I want to begin by exploring *The Beautiful Story* video released by the Church of England Evangelical Council (CEEC) in 2020 to coincide with the launch of Living in Love and Faith, the latest round of Anglican discussion around sexuality. The video attracted some controversy when it was released, but I believe it can helpfully be examined as a clear statement of conservative evangelical convictions on sexuality in the twenty-first century as evangelicals themselves choose to express them when wishing to commend them to others (primarily, as we shall see, to other evangelicals, but also to a wider audience).

Despite being a statement of conservative evangelical conviction on sexuality one of the surprising aspects of *The Beautiful Story* is the comparatively small amount of time that is devoted to discussing the interpretation of biblical passages. Despite continual insistence that scripture is very clear on this issue, there is a complete absence of any detailed discussion of the biblical passages that directly address sexuality. Instead, there is some discussion of the creation narratives as part of an argument that the consensus position is rooted in central themes of Christian belief. This argument, although clearly rooted in some exegetical points (man and woman are created equal but different) swiftly becomes abstracted from scripture to be expressed in much broader theological principles (male-female marriage reflects the life of the Trinity and our eternal destiny because it shows unity in difference) that are likely to have little traction with anyone who does not already accept a basic evangelical outlook. This underlines the fact that *The Beautiful Story* is not primarily addressed to non-evangelicals unfamiliar with their pattern of biblical interpretation. It is intended primarily for an internal audience who already understand the consensus position – they simply need to be reassured that it is true, and may need to be persuaded that it cannot be compromised. There is little time taken even here to justify an exegetical move the watcher is assumed to be familiar with from 'they shall become one flesh' to 'Christ will be united with his bride the church'.[1]

In fact, despite explicitly encouraging evangelicals to engage in the LLF process, the video shows a complete lack of interest in considering how to equip them to enter into a genuine dialogue with those who do not share evangelical presuppositions. At one point, in driving home the idea that evangelical interpretation of scripture is undoubtedly right, Ian Paul states that liberal scholars agree evangelicals are right in their interpretation of what scripture says, but simply refuse to obey scripture they believe is wrong.[2] Although this is clearly true of some scholars, there is no reference to the undeniable fact that many more progressive scholars sincerely believe evangelicals are misinterpreting scripture. This lazy caricature of non-conservative biblical interpretation, implicitly suggests that evangelicals are always faithful to scripture while liberals simply ignore scripture they disagree with, massively undermining any possibility of genuine dialogue.

A second striking aspect of *The Beautiful Story* is the apparent de-emphasis on addressing the issues of homophobia and injustice affecting gay people today – the topics that society at large regards as central to any discussion of sexuality and diversity. Although the video admits the church needs to repent of past failure, what exactly it needs to repent of is unclear – a single brief mention of homophobia is combined with a much more lengthy acknowledgement that the single life has been presented as a second-best option in evangelical churches. This conflation of the way the church may have failed gay people with the way it may have failed single people essentially de-emphasizes the seriousness of homophobia. The idea that single or partnered gay people might face prejudice or experience difficulties in church contexts simply because they are gay is never seriously explored. There is a lack of any recognition that some of the past homophobic failings of the church have included misinterpretation of scripture. Or that Christian homophobia might not entirely be a thing of the past, and might therefore prompt an ongoing need to critically examine our actions and attitudes. The one place where *The Beautiful Story* acknowledges that gay people might be in need of having a safe space where they can be celebrated and not crushed, and that providing these things might be an important part of Christian community is in its discussion of the risks for celibate gay people if the church were to change its policy. The idea that there might be gay people (celibate or otherwise) for whom these things are urgently needed now is completely absent.

As we noted in Chapter 1, evangelical writings in the Seventies explicitly acknowledged the reality that the traditional teaching and practice of the church in this area was profoundly homophobic and required repentance, that gay people (including gay Christians) experienced prejudice and injustice in wider society, and that churches were often not good at being supportive communities for them. Stott even noted that homophobia had led to mistranslation of Bible passages. This awareness of the church's homophobia and the present need of gay people for love, acceptance and support in a sometimes hostile world is significantly downplayed in *The Beautiful Story*. This is representative of an increasing tendency in recent writing to downplay the idea that the tradition of the church has been profoundly homophobic under the pressure of the need to assert that the consensus position represents faithfulness to an unchanged Christian tradition.

The third area that I wish to draw attention to in *The Beautiful Story* is the degree to which it was significantly politicized as a piece. Church politics (setting out the consequences of a change in church policy, the need for evangelical unity in order to oppose it, the 'red lines' that would cause people to leave, a consideration of forms of provision for dissenters and an appeal to pack General Synod with conservative candidates) took up a full 12 minutes of a 30 minute video. The assurances from Vaughan Roberts towards the end of the video that evangelicals don't want a culture war and aren't interested in politics but only the gospel seem hard to take seriously given the amount of space given to discussing politics. This is the section that occasioned some of the most significant criticism, as it seemed to represent evangelicals threatening the wider church with schism. Although there is clearly an extent to which the CEEC were seeking to send a warning shot across the bows of the church, it is probably best to understand this section (like the rest of the video) as primarily intended for an internal audience. Non-evangelicals are unlikely to be convinced by the rhetoric being used (as was obvious from the incomprehension with which some of it was met) and might even welcome the prospect of evangelical separation from the Church of England. It is to other evangelicals that much of this discussion was addressed.

Evangelicals were speaking to other evangelicals about what the prospect of a more progressive Church of England might mean for them. There were several obvious concerns here: first (a point often overlooked by critics of the video), CEEC clearly wanted to encourage evangelicals to continue to be loyal Anglicans and engage with the LLF process despite their reservations. They wanted to discourage pre-emptive jumping ship that might weaken the evangelical cause before key debates were even held. Second, it was important for the CEEC to reassure those conservatives convinced that this sort of engagement with the church might mean collusion with unfaithfulness that their concerns were heard. Third, and perhaps more importantly than either of these, the CEEC were obviously seeking to send a message to more progressive evangelicals who might be tempted to compromise. Such evangelicals were being warned that if they thought they could compromise on sexuality and still be considered a faithful evangelical, they were wrong. Key networks and respected leaders would leave the church and cut ties with those who stayed. Progressives who stayed would no longer be part of key networks, would be betraying the vulnerable, and would be outside the significant movement of the Spirit uniting evangelicals in mission that was warmly described in the video.

Part I – How has sexuality become a first order issue for evangelicals?

The analysis I have offered of *The Beautiful Story* highlights some of the key characteristics of the most recent evangelical discourse on sexuality: it is written for an internal evangelical audience and disinterested in seriously engaging with non-evangelical progressives; it tends to assume interpretation of biblical material is settled and rarely sees the need to re-engage with it; it downplays the reality of homophobia; and it functions politically to try to reassure conservatives they are in the right and to keep progressive evangelicals in line. It is political in the most straightforward sense: designed to achieve particular tactical ends rather than engage in an open way; and the political ends on which it is focused are actually primarily internal, directed within Anglican evangelicalism.

It is obvious that this way of discussing sexuality is quite different from the earliest evangelical writings, which may have been primarily directed at other evangelicals, but showed greater fluidity and transparency in their interpretation of scripture, engaged in constructive dialogue with those they disagreed with, and acknowledged evangelical complicity in homophobia. Clearly the general tone has moved from a position of at least moderate openness to one that is more defensive or even combative, with disagreement seen as a first order issue of faithfulness. Where discussion had once focused around the degree to which gay Christians could be included and celebrated within the church, with attention given to careful exegesis of scripture and to dealing with the realities of a homophobic culture in church and world, discussion now revolves around 'red lines' and the need to demonstrate faithfulness to the gospel, with tricky exegetical questions and considerations of gay welfare left unexplored or considered niche interests. To understand how and why the sexuality debate has become politicized in this way requires a deeper understanding of the history of British evangelicalism in the twentieth century. We can then set the sexuality debate in this wider context.

The evangelical Anglican identity crisis

At the beginning of the twentieth century the rising influence of modern liberal theology started to challenge the dominance of Victorian evangelicalism. As Stott would note in his introduction to *Issues Facing Christians Today* (1984): 'For approximately fifty years (c.1920–70) evangelicals were preoccupied with the task of defending the historic biblical faith against the attacks of liberalism, and reacting against its "social gospel".'[3] Stott's concern was that this preoccupation had prompted a neglect of evangelical concern for social justice, which he was a key figure in reversing, though the lingering suspicion of liberals would continue. The 50-year civil war he refers to took the form of a hugely divisive split within evangelicalism between the liberals (who prioritized a 'social gospel' of this-worldly mission), and the conservatives, who were concerned above all with evangelism and correct teaching on the cross. The split was literal in the case of some mission agencies, with BCMS (Bible Churchmen's Missionary Society, later Crosslinks) splitting from CMS (which would return to the evangelical fold by the end of the twentieth century) in 1922. Perhaps more consequentially, the Intervarsity Fellowship (now UCCF) also split from the Student Christian Movement around the same time. UCCF guarded its integrity as a conservative evangelical movement by defining itself in relation to its doctrinal basis. The experience shared by many Anglican evangelical church leaders of having served on the executive committee of a Christian Union in their formative years ties them directly into this historical inheritance, where doctrinal statements primarily function to police boundaries, acting as a means of guarding against liberal entryism. This model of evangelical identity implicitly suggests a disturbing vision of liberals: outwardly identical to faithful Christians, but fundamentally corrosive to the church's witness and unity, only able to be detected through their unwillingness to express their beliefs in the approved (and often forensically specific) wording of a doctrinal basis. This core element of shared evangelical identity establishes the conflictual nature of the church's existence in the world by defining themselves against an enemy within – the liberals – and encouraging the weaponization of doctrine as a way to expose and exclude them.

The movement Stott championed, to reverse this suspicious evangelical withdrawal from engagement with church and world, emerged in the Sixties, in the first National Evangelical Anglican Conference (NEAC) at Keele in 1967. The Keele conference signalled a newfound confidence within British evangelicalism, and represented a decisive turning point. The same period witnessed the emergence of the charismatic movement (the Fountain Trust was founded in 1964), which despite some initial suspicion would swiftly grow to become the dominant form of spirituality in modern evangelicalism. By the Nineties, there was a strong sense of triumphalism to the increasingly charismaticized evangelicalism expressed in key initiatives like Spring Harvest and the Alpha Course.

Alongside the triumph of evangelicalism in the church, however, went a growing realization that churchgoing as a whole was going through significant decline and many churches were closing. The wider movements of cultural change set in motion in the Sixties saw church and wider society drift further apart, until by the end of the twentieth century churchgoing was becoming a niche activity engaged in by a small and disproportionately elderly section of the population. Britain no longer felt like a Christian nation. For some evangelicals this represented a grave crisis that required fresh missional engagement with a changed world. For others it represented a purging of nominal or liberal believers that would result in a purer and more faithful church. Keele's vision of a confident Anglican evangelicalism re-engaging with the world therefore became an ambiguous one, capable of differing interpretations. For some it meant seeking to resist or undo the cultural influence of the Sixties and return church and culture to faithfulness. For others it meant consciously reinventing evangelicalism and what it meant to be church in the light of the new culture that was emerging out of the Sixties. The triumphant dynamism of the charismatic movement could colour either option – either proclaiming that the church would triumph over the forces of darkness in the world, or confidently engaging in creative celebration of wider culture. Both Greenbelt and March for Jesus were in their own ways expressions of evangelical confidence in the face of the modern world (and in the Eighties the same people might be involved in both, with little sense that they might express different outlooks on surrounding society).

During the second half of the twentieth century, key figureheads (such as John Stott, Nicky Gumbel, or the Baptist Steve Chalke), evangelical umbrella organizations (such as the Evangelical

Alliance or festivals such as Spring Harvest with its songbook), and resources (such as the Alpha Course or the publications of InterVarsity Press) created a superficial unity that concealed the growing divisions within evangelicalism. However, by the end of the twentieth century it was clear that there was no longer a shared evangelical identity, but instead multiple different ways of being an Anglican evangelical. Beyond the basic split between the March for Jesus conservatives and Greenbelt progressives suggested above, there were divisions between the charismatic and non-charismatic evangelicals, between those whose identity was more broad and Anglican than it was evangelical, and those whose Anglicanism was more of a flag of convenience on a basically non-denominational evangelicalism. The vote to ordain women at the end of the twentieth century brought some of these divisions out into the open. For the first time it became very clear that evangelicals were divided, with prominent evangelicals on both sides arguing their position on the basis of the authority of scripture.

This was the historical backdrop to the evangelical engagement with the sexuality debate.

Understanding the evangelical civil war

In the rest of this chapter we will examine the way in which evangelicals came to weaponize sexual ethics as a means of defining and redefining evangelical and Anglican identity, starting in the late Eighties, following the consolidation of the evangelical consensus position. The increasingly contested nature of evangelical Anglican identity during this period outlined above, forms the key backdrop to this process. Just as in a previous generation statements like UCCF's doctrinal basis became a key way to define evangelical identity, so adherence to the consensus position became a normative statement of what it meant to be evangelical.

In making this argument, I want to draw on some of the insights of the French-American philosopher Rene Girard.

Girard is particularly concerned with the unconscious mechanisms that motivate communities collectively in times of crisis, where a whole community can turn on a marginalized individual or group seemingly at random and turn them into the scapegoat for all their troubles. Girard's key insight here is that this mechanism comes into effect as a result of rising tensions and anxieties within a community, which focus on particular incidents that become scandalous, producing a level of outrage that is out of proportion with the actual events. Once a community has fastened its anxieties on a single incident like this, the community itself becomes scandalized, prone to taking offence and primed to find scapegoats. Scandalized communities become increasingly unable to recognize any clear-cut innocents, because irrespective of the rights and wrongs of any particular incident, all involved can be seen to be complicit in the generalized scandal, creating a 'no smoke without fire' effect. At the same time, because each incident is drawn into a wider pre-existing conflict, in which the community feel besieged, the community become increasingly unable to recognize their own guilt and complicity. Even when the community acts to attack others seemingly without provocation, they are able to point to the wrongs of the past as justification. When their perceived enemies seem to avoid aggression, this can always be interpreted as a provocative attempt to manoeuvre into a position of advantage while concealing their malicious intentions. The aggressor has always already been attacked, and the defender is always the one seeking confrontation.

It's also important to recognize that communities that become scandalized will inevitably begin to sense that their problems are caused by the actions of a single opponent – a rival behind all the conflict. Rivalry and the creation of scandals go naturally together – in allowing some incident to become a scandal (an incident somehow connected to other incidents), a community is also creating a rival (the enemy who acts against them in all cases). This rival may have some basis in reality, there may genuinely be an individual or group that oppose their interests. The key thing to recognize however, is that the rival being discerned in the context of a scandal is always more monstrous, more threatening, and less limited than any specific individual or group identified. This is in part because scandals become opportunistic – they attach themselves on to other smaller scandals around them, subordinating them to the bigger scandal, making the conflict far more complex and harder to resolve. In this way several small and apparently unrelated instances or grievances become linked in the mind of the community, creating a single huge scandal that somehow encompasses them all. The 'glue' in this process is the discerned involvement of a rival.

In the eyes of a scandalized community, their rival will increasingly be both nebulous (having an influence that can potentially be discerned anywhere) and monstrous (having a malign intent that is only partly expressed in any one incident). There is always an excess of outrage that attaches to any new scandal because the always-discerned presence of the rival links whatever offences have occurred in this incident with all of those that the rival is seen to be guilty of elsewhere. The guilt of those involved in the scandal is in part due to the fact that by their involvement they have necessarily been unmasked as agents of the monstrous rival. This perceived monstrousness of the rival encourages a rush to extremes, where increasingly violent and disproportionate responses to incidents can always be justified by reference to the already-assumed monstrousness of the rival. The community must become monstrous itself in order to defeat the monsters it sees opposing it. The logic is that of gang violence, where each outrage provokes an even greater atrocity in a fast-escalating vicious cycle. This is the dynamic that has led to the sort of rapid escalation of stakes that we see played out in more conservative evangelical circles in the late Nineties.

Scandalized communities

In the late Eighties and into the Nineties, Anglican evangelicals began to take on these characteristics of scandalized communities. To understand why this happened at this time requires reflecting on some of the events that occurred from 1984 (when Stott's *Issues Facing Christians Today* was published) to 1995 (when the CEEC published the St Andrew's Day Statement, asserting that sexuality was a first order issue of faith) and then into the new millennium.

The first thing to recognize is that in taking a firm stance against acceptance of same-sex relationships as equivalent to opposite-sex relationships, evangelicals were aligning themselves with a significant cultural movement pushing back against the legacy of the Sixties. Groups such as the Nationwide Festival of Light, founded in 1971 and Action for Biblical Witness to Our Nation (ABWON), founded in 1983, campaigned against the acceptability of queer sexualities and relationships in society, and found some support in the policies of Thatcher's Conservative government. When the 1988 Local Government Act including the infamous Section 28 was passed, conservative evangelical clergy and laity lobbied for it, making speeches in General Synod connecting church decline with the failure to take a serious moral lead against homosexuality. Figures such as Revd Tony Higton, chair of ABWON, campaigned for the church to take a more hardline stance, working in 1987 to eject LGCM from their offices on church property. The spread of the AIDS epidemic inspired a wave of homophobic sentiment in British society, encouraging the perception that gay people were diseased and immoral. The late Eighties represented a high point of social disapproval of gay relationships. In 1983 the British Social Attitudes survey had found that 50 per cent of the population thought gay relationships were always wrong. By 1987 the figure had risen to 64 per cent. They wouldn't return to the levels registered in 1983 until 1994, when they resumed a drift in a more permissive direction.[4]

The publication of the House of Bishops statement *Issues in Human Sexuality* in 1991 represented the evangelical George Carey's vision of a more Bible-centred church. For the first time, evangelicals could look to a Church of England report that was substantially in harmony with the consensus position. In 1992, the Church of England voted to ordain women as priests, in a move supported by many evangelicals. However, for a core group of conservative evangelicals the ordination of women represented a major battle lost against the legacy of the Sixties, with some evangelicals feeling they could not with integrity remain part of a church that had taken such a step. Reform was established the same year, explicitly to create a network for evangelicals in a semi-detached relationship with the wider church, defined partly on the grounds of their convictions on women's ministry, but also in their covenant defined by adherence to the consensus position on sexuality. This was one of the first clear signs of the fragmentation of evangelical identity. The conservative evangelical Gerald Bray was to write in an editorial in *The Churchman* in 1993:

> Convinced evangelicals are now derided as 'narrow' by those who are more 'open', and are being consistently marginalized within their own constituency ... It is worth reflecting that if Jesus had been an 'open evangelical' there would not be a church at all today.[5]

Alongside this, but perhaps less recognized, was a corresponding reassessment of Anglican evangelical identity on the part of progressives. For a group of progressive evangelicals who had campaigned for the ordination of women, the open opposition of conservative evangelicals (and the subsequent decision on the part of some to distance themselves from the mainstream of the church, disinheriting progressives as not true evangelicals) had shattered any sense of evangelical unity. Many of these progressive evangelicals had been campaigning for the ordination of women alongside liberals, and would now continue to find common cause with them in campaigning groups such as GRAS and WATCH. For some, this meant abandoning 'evangelical' as an identity altogether. The popularity of Dave Tomlinson's book *The Post Evangelical* in 1995 was not coincidental – it struck a chord with many who were dissatisfied with a tightly controlled conservative evangelical definition of what an evangelical identity looked like.

By the Nineties then, it is clear that Anglican evangelicals were a fractured community with significant tensions caused by competing visions of what it meant to be an evangelical in the modern world. In the final years of the twentieth century, conservative evangelicals became increasingly politicized, seeking to stand against any compromise on sexuality. A series of scandalous incidents started to create a certainty among conservatives that a monstrous rival was mobilizing against them in both church and world. The election of New Labour in 1997 signalled a liberal shift in the public mood. The British Social Attitudes survey in 2000 showed only 37 per cent thought same-sex relationships were always wrong, and 34 per cent thought they weren't wrong at all. A succession of progressive government policies brought increased tolerance and legal rights for gay people within wider society, up to and including moves towards the criminalization of discrimination on the grounds of sexuality. In 2000 the ban on LGBT service in the armed forces was lifted. In 2002 gay couples were able to adopt children. In the same year, when the liberal catholic Rowan Williams (known to be pro-gay) was nominated to replace George Carey as Archbishop of Canterbury, this was actively opposed by conservative evangelicals arguing he was heretical. The very next year, in 2003, a similar battle was waged successfully against the appointment of Jeffrey John as Bishop of Oxford. Later that same year Section 28 was repealed. In 2004 the Civil Partnership Act was passed, allowing same-sex couples access to an equivalent legal status to married couples. The Church of England guidance published the following year stressed that such unions could not be recognized as marriages by the church, but allowed for clergy to enter into them and advised that those within such partnerships should be fully accepted within church congregations. By 2007 this changed legal landscape was part of what prompted the foundation of the Christian Legal Centre to provide pro bono legal support for Christians discriminated against on behalf of their faith.

The changing public mood fuelled a sense among conservative evangelicals that they were under attack. The CEEC St

Andrew's Day statement of 1995, despite being framed as an invitation to dialogue with liberal scholars on the issue of sexuality, was clearly intended by at least some of the signatories to be a robust statement of the consensus position as a first order issue on which evangelicals could unite. When LGCM held a service of thanksgiving at Southwark Cathedral in 1996, it was loudly opposed by both ABWON and Reform, with Anne Atkins condemning it on Radio 4's Thought for the Day. In 1998, following well-organized conservative lobbying, Resolution 1.10 of the Lambeth conference, which had been framed to condemn homophobia, was amended to include the statement that homosexual practice was incompatible with scripture.

Some of the above could be viewed as unprovoked acts of aggression on the part of conservative evangelicals, though from within the scandalized community they would be perceived as defensive reactions, because the aggressor has always already been attacked, and individual incidents become merged into an overall scandal within scandalized communities. All of this frames any individual incident – any scandal is also about all the other scandals. Scandalized conservative evangelicals were therefore convinced of their own innocence even while acting in aggressive ways.

Monstrous rivals

During the Nineties, conservative writing on sexuality became increasingly combative and less pastorally focused, partly driven by a growing awareness that they were facing a monstrous rival. This was the period when evangelical amnesia about the history of the consensus position began to set in. Increasingly, the sense that the consensus position was based on a relatively recent pattern of biblical interpretation was forgotten, as was the sense in which it represented a change from a historically homophobic church tradition. Statements of pastoral concern for gay people and condemnation of homophobia became increasingly perfunctory, and reference to the church's need to repent of past homophobia disappeared entirely. There were two key influences behind this change: a charismatic-inspired focus on spiritual warfare, and stronger links to North American writing that was influenced by the culture wars of the States. Both would also start to give a plausible shape to the emerging evangelical understanding of their monstrous rival.

The first of these is best illustrated by reference to John White's *Eros Redeemed*, published in 1993 as a thoroughly revised and expanded version of his earlier *Eros Defiled*. *Eros Defiled* had presented a conservative approach to sexuality, but with a strong pastoral tone. In *Eros Redeemed*, White thoroughly recasts his whole approach to sexual morality in the light of spiritual warfare – presenting sexual sin as the key battleground against demonic forces, drawing on Romans 1 to present homosexuality itself (and AIDS in particular) as a sign of God's judgement on the West: 'Sexual sin in the church may be the single greatest obstacle to the church's evangelistic impact on the world. Certainly our sexual enslavement is a prime goal of Satan's.'[6] Acceptance of homosexual activity meant collusion with the forces of darkness, and signalled acceptance of false teaching and the exaltation of the self and its interests and judgements. Manifestly, this is an outlook that discourages moderation or the creation or preservation of a middle ground – once sexuality has been understood as an issue of spiritual warfare such things become viewed as concessions to the enemy. It should also be recognized that the imagery of spiritual warfare was not entirely distinct from the rhetoric of culture wars. The culture wars in the US were frequently regarded as a spiritual conflict, with sexuality as a spiritual as well as political battleground, where the progressive side is aligned with the forces of darkness.

If *Eros Redeemed* suggested that the growing charismatic tradition had the potential to pull evangelicals towards a more conservative position, it was not the only influence. The culture wars of the US in the Nineties produced a new standard work on sexuality for conservative evangelicals in Thomas E. Schmidt's *Straight & Narrow?* published in a UK edition by

InterVarsity Press in 1995. Although Schmidt went out of his way to argue against homophobia and to call evangelicals to costly love for gay people, this message was drowned out by some of his other emphases. Schmidt argued that there was a 'gay movement' actively working in culture and politics to promote same-sex relationships as an expression of a different, non-Christian, way of life that undermined marriage and the heterosexual family, which it saw as oppressive. Alongside this ideological threat he argued that homosexuality was inherently promiscuous: 'promiscuity among homosexual men is not a mere stereotype, and it is not merely the majority experience – it is virtually the only experience ... there is practically no comparison possible to heterosexual marriage'.[7] He argued gay sexual practice posed serious health risks:

> No honest look at current scientific research allows us to view homosexual practice as peaceable and harmless. For the vast majority of homosexual men, and for a significant number of homosexual women – even apart from the deadly plague of AIDS – sexual behaviour is obsessive, psychopathological and destructive to the body.[8]

He even went as far as to suggest links to paedophilia:

> One other concern that merits attention is the disproportionate number of male homosexuals who prefer sex with boys ... the problem is compounded by the fact that many paedophiles deny that it is a problem and demand full inclusion in the homosexual liberation movement.[9]

The influence of this sense of the monstrousness of gay people can be seen in the third edition of Stott's *Issues Facing Christians Today* in 1999, which saw some significant editing of Stott's original Eighties text. For the first time Stott asserted that homosexuality was an issue on which there could be no compromise or tolerance of diversity because faithfulness to the gospel was at stake. Referencing Schmidt, Stott also began to emphasize the health risks of gay sex and to talk about the inherent promiscuity in a 'gay lifestyle'.[10] Although he continued to affirm that gay relationships were genuinely loving, it was clear he was now presenting them as intrinsically non-comparable to straight relationships. Finally, Stott seemed to move in the direction of a more explicit statement about the existence of a gay-liberal conspiracy, positing that the 1973 decision of the American Psychiatric Association to remove homosexuality from its official list of mental illnesses was entirely the result of the political lobbying by a 'liberal conspiracy'.[11] Further editorial changes suggested that all 'homosexual Christians' (apparently seen as constituting a single uniformly liberal group) could be described as 'not satisfied' with biblical teaching and the institution of heterosexual marriage.[12]

Stott remained the key figure for mainstream evangelical thinking in the Nineties, and this acceptance on his part of the rhetoric of a gay-liberal conspiracy represented a significant shift of the middle ground in a conservative direction. The perception that evangelicals were being opposed by a monstrous rival, who could plausibly be seen as always already the aggressor in any situation became an ever-present undertone. This combined a politicized outlook derived from the culture wars of the US with the imagery of spiritual warfare to present an image of a monstrous rival who worked to destroy society from within and was secretly behind changes in the stances of institutions.

The Evangelical Alliance's 1998 statement *Faith, Hope and Homosexuality* stressed the existence of an ever more powerful gay lobby in wider society described as constituting part of a cultural movement 'away from absolutes based on biblical revelation, to judgements based on self-determination, self-fulfilment and individual rights'.[13] By contrast, evangelicals were seen as genuinely vulnerable to persecution under discrimination legislation because of their faith. The statement effectively reframed what the issue at stake in the debate around sexuality was. It was assumed a Christian position on sexuality was already clear. Rather than seeking further discernment, the task was to consider how an increasingly vulnerable church should respond to a large and powerful liberal conspiracy seeking to normalize sinful patterns of sexual behaviour.

By the late Nineties, it is clear that conservative evangelicals were a scandalized community, constantly provoked by the acts of a monstrous rival (even if these were as innocuous as holding a thanksgiving service for a Christian organization that had existed for 20 years). In their own eyes they were always the wronged party, even when engaging in seemingly unprovoked acts of aggression.

The fracturing of evangelical unity on sexuality

In the Nineties, conservative evangelicals began to insist that sexuality was a first order issue. For progressive evangelicals (often interested in engaging in dialogue with non-evangelicals), the insistence that debate on this area could now no longer be tolerated was problematic. For charismatics (characteristically more interested in activism than finer points of doctrine), the insistence that forensic detection of heresy in the statements made by other believers was now a priority was problematic. As the Nineties progressed, it became increasingly clear that not all evangelicals were willing to adopt an understanding that the consensus position was a first order issue.

One of the earliest examples of this within Anglican evangelicalism came in 1995 when Michael Vasey, liturgy tutor at the evangelical theological college Cranmer Hall, and a member of the evangelical group on General Synod, published *Strangers and Friends*. Commissioned by the patronage secretary of the evangelical Church Pastoral Aid Society (who was then refused permission to endorse it), it became emblematic of the threat of a liberal 'enemy within' for some evangelicals. The book was seen as significant enough that it was discussed at multiple points by Stott in the third edition of *Issues Facing Christians Today*, with Stott describing it as a 'sincere but misguided attempt ... to combine evangelical faith with homosexual advocacy'.[14] Vasey followed the approach that until 1990 had been the official line of the Church of England, in asserting that the biblical material directly addressing homosexuality was largely irrelevant to the modern situation. Instead he made a case for an ethics of pastoral pragmatism, drawing on the broad resources of scripture (in particular he recommended an engagement with biblical material on friendship) to offer support to a vulnerable gay community. Vasey explicitly wrote as an evangelical looking to scripture for inspiration, but he was transparently seeking to demolish the idea that the consensus position alone represented faithful obedience to scripture. The response to the book was a clear sign that, faced with an enemy within, the diversity on interpretation and flexibility of approach seen within evangelical writing in the Seventies could no longer be tolerated. The EA mounted a campaign against the book. Reform demanded that Vasey be sacked, and when he was not, 'blacklisted' Cranmer Hall as a theological training college.

By the end of the millennium, it was clear that adherence to the consensus position as a first order issue was drawing lines of gospel faithfulness between factions within Anglican evangelicalism as well as around its external boundaries, and that this was resulting in a thorough politicization of writing on sexual ethics. Although Cranmer Hall was the first evangelical TEI to be blacklisted by conservative evangelicals it wasn't the last. Evangelical churches and networks would increasingly be involved in blacklisting of colleges, withholding payments of diocesan share and declaring themselves in impaired communion with their bishops over issues of sexuality. In the new millennium this tendency would accelerate, with Anglican evangelicals increasingly working to build alternative networks and structures in parallel to those of the Church of England, a process that would be given formal justification at the Global Anglican Future Conference in Jerusalem in 2008.

Part II – Where does this leave us?

The rush to extremes

By the Nineties it is clear that conservative evangelicals were discerning a monstrous rival in the form of a gay-liberal conspiracy as the guiding force behind a string of apparently unrelated incidents. This conflated secular gay rights activists, groups like the LGCM, pro-gay cultural products in the media, the nebulous effects of dark spiritual forces, and progressive evangelicals questioning the consensus position into a single monstrous enemy. Those caught up in the scandalized community assigned blame to the gay-liberal conspiracy collectively, and could hold any member of this group responsible for the worst excesses of any other member. Michael Vasey whose evangelical credentials were impeccable, but who was gay and questioned the consensus position, could therefore quite easily appear monstrous and utterly different from evangelicals within the scandalized community.

It's important to recognize here that Girard's analysis makes clear the creation of a monstrous other by scandalized communities is a *mirrored* and mutual process. The rapid demonization of a gay-liberal conspiracy by conservatives around the turn of the millennium has been accompanied by a parallel demonization of a fundamentalist and homophobic evangelical church by progressives. In 2000 LGCM published a report on Christian homophobia, documenting the modern persecution of gay and lesbian couples by the church. Many activists for gay rights had powerful testimonies of the homophobia they had experienced within evangelical communities, often as vulnerable young people wrestling with their own sexual identity, including attempted exorcisms, conversion therapy, and expulsion from positions of responsibility or from church communities as a whole. The rhetoric of evangelicals as a homophobic monstrous other, talking about 'loving the sinner' while excluding gay people and regarding them as a threat, and blindly adhering to a fundamentalist faith of biblical literalism, became a commonplace of progressive rhetoric. In 2005 the ethicist Andrew Linzey edited jointly with Richard Kirker of LGCM a volume of progressive responses to the proposed Windsor Report on managing divisions in the Anglican Communion. In his introduction, Linzey argued passionately that the Church of England as a whole, and evangelicals and conservative Catholics in particular, were profoundly homophobic, expressing a thoroughgoing aversion to gay people that he paralleled with executions of gay people during the holocaust.[15]

In 2011, Symon Hill, associate director of the Christian thinktank Ekklesia, went on a pilgrimage to repent of Christian homophobia and his own previous complicity in it. Prior to this, he gave an address on Christianity and homophobia to the Camden LGBT Forum, in which he made it clear that he saw much of the church (explicitly naming the evangelical-dominated Anglican Mainstream and Christian Concern) as bigoted and homophobic:

> Much of the church is, to one extent or another, homophobic. This homophobia is perpetuated by bigots who define their faith by their hatred of gay people and by liberals who fail to speak up for inclusion out of a misplaced desire for unity.[16]

This last comment is clearly a veiled reference to Rowan Williams. These examples make clear that progressives have also created a monstrous other, which links evangelicals, conservative Catholics, historic pre-modern homophobia, Anglican provinces in the global South supporting actively homophobic government policies, the holocaust, the deeply traumatic experiences of individual activists, and ersatz liberals who do not make full use of their agency to bring the change progressives seek. As with the conservative monstrous other, any member of the group can be held responsible for the worst excesses of any other member, so that Rowan Williams, whose pro-gay credentials are impeccable, could quite easily appear monstrous and utterly different from the scandalized community.

In regard to both the monstrous rivals it is important to recognize that the perception of the other is both true and not true. It is undoubtedly the case that both conservatives and progressives have genuinely acted monstrously at various points. Individual instances of provocative overreaction, persecution and exclusion can be identified. However, no single progressive or conservative is guilty of or reducible to the entirety of what the monstrous other is perceived to be. It is likewise true that there are progressives and conservatives who actively seek the best for the other. However, these complex realities become harder to acknowledge (and to inhabit) the more that the myth of the monstrous other dominates the imagination. Instead, there is a pressure created that provokes ever more extreme responses because the outrage caused by all of those identified as part of the monstrous other can be focused on any individual identified as part of it. Any individual who is categorized as monstrous can justifiably be responded to in a monstrous manner. So the young person who comes out as gay in a conservative evangelical setting might be reacted to as if this means they are espousing liberal theology and challenging the authority of the church leaders, or as if they are seeking to undermine the moral fabric of society. Similarly, the university CU member attending a progressive church who tries to publicize a mission event might be reacted to as if this means they are personally responsible for a prominent gay Christian having been put through conversion therapy, or as if they hold to an essentially pre-modern faith. Defensive overreactions, excluding people from leadership positions or friendships, or even explicitly or implicitly forcing them out of the church can be easily justified by reference to things *known to be true* of the monstrous other even if no attempt has been made to establish if they are true of this particular person.

The collapse of the middle ground

Although I have set out clearly the extent to which both sides, conservatives and progressives, are almost identical in their mirroring behaviour, it is important to recognize that the creation of a monstrous other is precisely the point when those within the scandalized communities can only see how utterly different they are. The scandalized groups drive the fracturing of the very communities that they ostensibly seek to protect by taking a firm stand against the enemy within. Middle ground and mediating positions become increasingly difficult to find, as each side can see only how utterly different the other is. The pressure this places on those like Vasey and Williams who seek to create mediating positions (evangelical *and* progressive, progressive *and* unifying) is immense. Neither side wants to acknowledge the existence or even possibility of middle ground. You are either with them, or part of the monstrous other. Anyone who continues to inhabit the ambiguous position of being both 'of us' and yet also 'of them' will inevitably be scapegoated. British evangelicals have seen a number of such scapegoats over the years, with the prominent Baptist Steve Chalke perhaps being the most prominent. Chalke was one of the most prominent evangelicals in the UK, being a well-known figure in the media for his work with his Oasis Trust, and was closely associated with the Evangelical Alliance and the Spring Harvest festival. In 2013 he published an article in *Christianity* magazine affirming his support for monogamous same-sex relationships. The move prompted widespread rejection of Chalke and his ministry in evangelical circles. He and the Oasis Trust were repudiated by the EA, and pressure mounted on the Baptist Federation to take action against him.

In evangelical circles the exclusion of the middle ground placed increasing bifurcatory pressure on those like John Stott who were seeking to be moderate figures of evangelical unity. Conservative evangelicals insisted sexuality was a first order issue, that the Bible was very clear and supported a traditional understanding held for centuries, stressed the myth of the gay-liberal conspiracy, and downplayed pastoral concern for gay people. Progressive evangelicals were increasingly dissatisfied with this. Some wanted to be more open about the complexity of the issue, others wanted the freedom to interpret texts differently in dialogue with non-evangelicals, and many were concerned about homophobia among evangelicals and wanted to re-emphasize that pastoral needs might mean that accommodation and flexibility was necessary. The two positions were set out clearly in two books from the US that were highly influential on British evangelicals. In 1998 the American ethicist Stanley J. Grenz's *Welcoming But Not Affirming: An Evangelical Response to Homosexuality* presented the consensus position but with a rather progressive spin to it. He accepted that faithful Christians might adopt a variety of views, implicitly accepting that sexuality was not a first order issue, rejected the myth of the gay-liberal conspiracy, and argued for Christians to work to promote equal rights for gay people in wider society. A few years later the American biblical scholar Robert Gagnon published *The Bible and Homosexual Practice* in 2001, presenting the consensus position with a conservative spin. He argued that homosexuality was linked to paedophilia and promiscuity, posed a threat to society and to gay people themselves, and asserted the existence of a gay-liberal conspiracy working actively to conceal these facts and persecute conservatives. He argued that sexually active gay people should be treated as unrepentant sinners, and excluded from the church community.

The difficulty of stating the consensus position in a way that would resonate with both conservative and progressive evangelicals when their positions were becoming increasingly opposed was made clear in the fourth and final edition of Stott's *Issues Facing Christians Today*, published in 2006 and co-written with Roy McCloughrey. This edition featured a significant rewrite of the sexuality section, reflecting competing influences from both progressives and conservatives. The biblical material remained largely unchanged, but (seemingly under implicit progressive influence) the tone of acceptance of gay people and a gay identity was strengthened throughout. For the first time, the reality of persecution of gay people was spelled out, with an implicit argument that Christians should seek to protect their rights – with reference to countries where same-sex relationships were punished by death and the full humanity of gay people was not recognized. However, this progressive emphasis was almost completely undermined by the rewrite of the discussion of AIDS under apparent conservative influence. Ever since first including reference to AIDS in the second edition, Stott had clearly stated that AIDS was not a specifically 'gay plague'. Now this was changed to the claim:

> Although we may not be able to say that HIV/AIDS is God's judgement on any particular individual, we can say that if a society tolerates wrongdoing and even celebrates it by calling 'evil good and good evil' then it must face up to the consequences of doing so (Romans 1.18–32).[17]

This theological gloss, alongside the description of the health risks of gay sex, assertion of gay promiscuity, and statement that homosexuality was a first order issue that were introduced in the third edition, suggested that the persecuted gay people whose human rights evangelicals should be defending were in fact diseased, immoral and a threat to the health of society, that society's tolerance of their sexual behaviour was bringing divine judgement upon us, and that maintaining a firm line on the issue was of creedal importance. The pressure that the consensus position was coming under from both sides had strained it almost to breaking point. It was becoming almost impossible to state an evangelical position on sexuality that would keep both conservatives and progressives on board. Moving forward, evangelicals on both sides would stop even making the attempt to do so.

Redrawing the lines – progressive evangelicals versus conservative evangelicals

Over the first two decades of the twenty-first century an increasing number of progressive evangelicals on both sides of the Atlantic would attempt to stake out new positions on sexuality. A typical example was Justin Lee's 2013 *Unconditional: Rescuing the Gospel from the Gays-vs-Christians Debate*, which highlighted the damage caused to people, relationships, and the gospel by the culture wars over sexuality. Lee appealed for evangelicals to commit to unconditional acceptance of gay people and acknowledge that we do not have the levels of certainty in our understandings of sexuality and scripture to be making the sort of divisive arguments we are making. Other progressive evangelicals would tackle the question of biblical interpretation head on, arguing that the consensus position did not represent the best or only interpretation of the key texts. James Brownson, an American Reformed minister and biblical scholar, published his *Bible, Gender, Sexuality* in 2013. It was an in-depth scholarly discussion of the central biblical texts that explicitly aimed to refute Gagnon's 2001 work that had become the central statement of the conservative position. In 2014 Matthew Vines, an American gay evangelical published a popular-level book *God and the Gay Christian*, designed to bring together a synthesis of the strongest progressive arguments on the biblical text and explicitly aimed at convincing American evangelicals to change their minds and become pro-gay activists. In 2020 David Runcorn, a British evangelical Anglican, published *Love Means Love* as a contribution to the Church of England's Living in Love and Faith discussions. It explicitly addressed faithful Bible-believing evangelicals who had found themselves in church contexts where a party line was being imposed that they felt uncomfortable with but unable to challenge. In 2022, Steven Croft's *Together in Love and Faith* explicitly made an evangelical case for the adoption of same-sex marriage in the Church of England.

A hallmark of all these progressive evangelical writings is their very explicit commitment to the authority of scripture, and their willingness to state that the key biblical texts simply cannot be read with the degree of certainty that conservatives suggest they can. The position on biblical interpretation of the key passages being argued for in all of these cases broadly corresponds to Bailey's judgement that the biblical passages that directly address homosexuality are culture-bound and cannot be directly applied to our modern situation (Brownson's position is slightly more nuanced, but he starts by disallowing a direct application of the key texts). Notably, however, having concluded that scripture gives no direct instruction, the theology progressive evangelicals then construct from elsewhere in scripture varies widely. In most cases the position argued for is far more liberal than Bailey's. Where he did not hesitate to see homosexuality as being less than God's perfect intention for humanity, most of these writers are insistent that gay sexuality should be fully affirmed as perfectly expressing the image of God.

The variety of alternative understandings being presented here mean that progressive evangelicals do not in any sense represent an alternate consensus. Progressive evangelicals tend to represent individualized readings of scripture that have little in common beyond their rejection of the consensus position. Many draw freely on the insights of non-evangelical progressive writers on the subject (whose approach to biblical authority they may not share). The lack of any recognized middle ground between the two scandalized communities makes maintaining an identity that is both evangelical and progressive difficult. This may not concern conservatives, but it points to future difficulties for the sustainability of a progressive evangelical identity.

Redrawing the lines – conservative evangelicals versus progressive evangelicals

On the other side of the divide, conservatives were similarly moving away from the prevarication of insisting on the need to defend the rights of people who many of them saw as part of a gay-liberal conspiracy to destroy marriage. The Archbishop of Canterbury's 2004 letter to the Primates, reiterating the need for a moderation of language due to the real persecution faced by homosexuals worldwide prompted an open letter to the *Sunday Times* in response from Reform which stated that this was 'presumably a gesture to the gay community who love to peddle this line that they all feel under enormous pressure and they are all being persecuted which is not true'.[18] There was likewise a move away from debating points of biblical interpretation of the traditional passages with liberal scholars who they felt rejected the authority of scripture. These twin tendencies – to downplay homophobia and to move away from dialogue on biblical interpretation – are both clearly on display in *The Beautiful Story*. With the de-emphasis on these areas, conservative evangelical writing has become more internalized and politicized – ultimately directed towards resourcing conservatives rather than engaging with the wider church.

In these tendencies the two influences we identified earlier (the influence of the charismatic movement and of the culture wars of the US) are still discernable. The move to de-emphasize a concern with homophobia and the intricacies of biblical interpretation reflect a charismatic move towards action and away from reflection. The origins of this tendency can be seen back in the Nineties in the way in which the Alpha Course addresses sexuality. The course material itself steers clear of controversial topics and never addresses sexuality, but Gumbel addresses homosexuality in his 1994 book *Searching Issues*, intended as supporting material for the course. Unsurprisingly, Gumbel presents the consensus position, explicitly referencing Stott for his understanding of the biblical material and White for his approach to pastoral issues. However, for Gumbel it is clear that the key issue for Christians was whether they were obedient to scripture, whose meaning is assumed to already be clear: 'Jesus took the Scriptures as his authority and if Jesus is our Lord, then we must follow him.'[19] Gumbel showed little desire to open up complex questions around biblical interpretation and addressing homophobia in the church, preferring instead to focus on the need for the believer to respond in simple obedience and clear action. Homophobia is never mentioned. In contrast to Stott's attempt to tortuously hold the extremes together, Gumbel adopts a different strategy – downplaying the sexuality debate altogether. HTB has notably followed this strategy ever since, making brief and formulaically conservative statements where necessary, but being markedly reluctant to give the issue prominence or to speak out politically.[20]

The influence of the culture wars of the US also continued to be felt. The move towards a largely internalized conversation that is mainly concerned with resourcing conservatives also had a specifically political dimension, as illustrated by *God, Gays and the Church,* published in 2007. This book, edited by Lisa Nolland, Chris Sugden and Sarah Finch (all closely associated with Anglican Mainstream – Sugden was its executive secretary), was produced in response to an acrimonious debate on homosexuality in the Church of England's General Synod earlier that year, in which conservatives felt that their position had not been heard. A compendium of resources for the sexuality debate, it included testimonies from the US ex-gay movement and extensive extracts from people involved in corrective treatment for homosexuality. Gay culture was presented as inherently promiscuous, and facilitating paedophilia, with several contributors declaring that lifelong and exclusive same-sex partnerships analogous to marriage were a myth within an inherently promiscuous gay culture. Nolland suggested that activist groups like Changing Attitude hid behind 'safe' gay figureheads such as Jeffrey John who advocated either celibacy or same-sex marriage, but that their real agenda was: 'concessionary infidelity legitimated by the therapeutic, even Christian, imperative for self-actualization and "personal growth" … and "brief and loving sexual engagement between mature adults in special circumstances" as "occasions of grace"'.[21] Ultimately, she suggested, they sought to undermine any ideal of exclusivity in sexual relationships, either gay or straight, with the end goal of destroying marriage as an institution. This is an extreme example, but the tendency towards the publication of books that acted to further fuel a polarized debate, rather than attempts to engage in genuine dialogue with those who disagreed, was more widespread.

A prominent example of conservative publications aimed at resourcing a debate is Glyn Harrison's 2014 *A Better Story: God, Sex, and Human Flourishing* which is perhaps best understood as a resource for conservatives struggling to communicate the consensus position. Harrison discussed the way cultural change since the Sixties had stopped a traditional presentation of the authority of scripture from making sense. Instead, he argued that teaching about sexuality should be approached as an exercise in apologetics: presenting the consensus position becomes synonymous with sharing the good news. Harrison's approach takes the conviction that the consensus position is a first order of faith for granted – it is not a position that needs to be argued for with careful exegesis of biblical passages, simply a truth that must be accepted. This has two key implications. First, that those who do not already hold to the consensus position are effectively in need of the gospel. And, second, that the consensus position itself is so core a doctrinal truth that the entire gospel can be retold around it: 'far from being a personal matter, issues of sex and the ordering of sexual relationships sit at the heart of God's big picture for the life of the world'.[22]

It is *A Better Story* that provides the blueprint for *The Beautiful Story*'s approach of avoiding any discussion of the biblical texts that directly address homosexuality, and focusing instead on a grand narrative of human flourishing that is rooted in an exposition of Genesis 1 and 2. For conservatives the appeal of this approach is obvious – rather than having to debate obscure passages in the sort of detail that would reveal that they are not straightfoward to interpret, they can focus on passages whose meaning is far clearer and which are far more central to the core gospel message in the certainty that accepting them is tantamount to accepting the consensus position.

At a time when progressive evangelicals were increasingly seeking to return to detailed questions of biblical interpretation, dissatisfied with conservative insistence that only one interpretation was possible and that it had to be accepted as a first order matter, conservatives were therefore denying that there was anything left to debate, and framing the whole debate as about the acceptance of the gospel as a whole. The reframing of a conservative approach away from the forensic focus on questions of biblical interpretation than had once been its hallmark, and towards seeing teaching on sexuality as synonymous with preaching the gospel, both discouraged genuine dialogue with anyone who didn't hold to their interpretation, and disempowered anyone in conservative congregations from asking questions about it. *The Beautiful Story* displays all of this – enthusiastically embraced by conservatives as a positive statement of the consensus position that avoids dwelling on divisive areas to present a call to unity round the cause of the gospel, it was rejected by progressives who saw it as a retreat into literalist certainty and a refusal to allow genuine dialogue.

Apocalypse or the kingdom

The rush to polarized extremes that seems to be the hallmark of the sexuality debate might be assumed to only end one way – in violent conflict and the irretrievable breakdown of communities. As progressives and conservatives increasingly view each other through the lens of the monstrous other they have created and mediating positions become impossible to maintain, a split of some sort seems unavoidable. Given the way in which both sides have now allied themselves with other provinces of the Anglican Communion worldwide, a formal split in the Church of England would likely also have the effect of legitimizing the current splits and fractures in the wider Communion, where conservative groupings operate across provincial boundaries and in impaired communion with Canterbury.

However, Girard would argue that this is only one possibility. Although to those embroiled within the conflict the utter difference of the monstrous other is obvious in all areas, to those able to view the conflict from the outside it is immediately obvious how almost identical the rivals are. Progressives and conservatives have far more in common than either are willing to admit. A surprising number of leading progressives are former conservatives. Both are self-evidently passionately committed to the cause of the gospel, to the defence of the vulnerable, and to the future of the church in the modern world, even if they approach those things very differently. Both are complicit in the fear, hatred, violence and exclusion that has been created by their conflict. Although none of them can shoulder all the blame for the works of the monstrous other, all have a share in some of it.

This commonality means that the rush to some sort of resolution could have a different outcome – instead of each side seeking to destroy the other they see as utterly different it could be a moment where they realize their sameness. Seeing your own monstrousness in the eyes of the other can spark utter rejection or it could be the doorway to an unimagined reconciliation. It may only be possible to really see ourselves in both our monstrousness and our beauty if we can see it through the eyes of another. Indeed, this is one plausible way of understanding Paul's encounter with Christ on the Damascus Road – he saw the true monstrosity of his persecution of the followers of the way by seeing himself through the eyes of the crucified Messiah. These moments of conflict give us that opportunity, if we are willing to be open to it. This could be a tragedy or a comedy. Until the denouement no one knows which it will be. We are headed either to apocalypse or the kingdom of God.

There are signs that, in the midst of the hardening of positions and rush to extremes, there are also some moves towards greater self-understanding on the part of conservatives and a willingness to recognize that they have been too narrow and inflexible in their thinking. This comes across in the section of *The Beautiful Story* that I mentioned earlier – where the failures of conservatives to make space for single people within church communities is highlighted. Although in the video this is unhelpfully conflated with the need to address homophobia, the reason this connection is made is because it is single gay conservatives who have raised the issue. Ed Shaw (who prefers the term 'same-sex attracted') raised the question sharply in his 2015 *The Plausibility Problem*. He pointed out that conservative declarations that they 'love the sinner but hate the sin' are rendered implausible if the lived experience of any gay Christian is that the church doesn't know how to support them and is unwilling to make the slightest change to their largely families-and-children oriented practice in order to do so.

Shaw's is only the most prominent of a number of contributions to the debate from gay conservatives, who are increasingly becoming prominent. It is easy for progressives to disregard this as tokenistic, but there is a clear sense that these voices bring a different perspective, helping conservatives recognize that there are real people at the centre of these debates, not just figures with symbolic value in a culture war. It is notable that prominent gay conservative voices have often done much within conservative evangelicalism to prevent a slide into the worst extremes of homophobia. The earliest British evangelical publication on the subject of sexuality was *The Returns of Love* a first-person account of a conservative gay Christian written by the pseudonymous Alex Davidson and published by InterVarsity Press in 1970. It had a significant influence on Stott, who cites it in *Issues Facing Christians Today*. Similarly, the publication of Alex Tyree's *Walking with Gay Friends* by InterVarsity Press in 2007 could be seen as a response to the harder line being presented by figures like Gagnon in 2001.

None of these books make a case for a progressive approach. All take for granted that gay Christians should live a single life and practise sexual abstinence. But none of them advocate for any form of 'healing' ministry or suggest that they expect their orientation to change. None of them suggest that homophobia is illusory or insignificant. Simply by speaking they make the case that conservatives need to imagine a church in which the presence of faithful gay Christians is a permanent reality. Both Shaw and Tyree are openly critical of evangelical attempts to pay lip-service to the need to offer pastoral support to gay people, and robust in their acknowledgement that this is common. Both advocate for the need for evangelical churches to change their culture in order to give the affirmation that gay Christians need, rather than offering a reluctantly tolerated place as those who have not been blessed by being straight. The increased openness to gay voices in conservative evangelical approaches is therefore an interesting development that may signal an openness to change and self-reflection.

Conclusion: Simplistic answers to complex questions

The sexuality debate in the church has become highly politicized in evangelical thinking and writing because it has become scandalized, in Girard's terms. Discussions around sexuality act as lightning rods for fears and tension around evangelical identity. Throughout the second half of the twentieth century evangelicalism has become steadily more fractured. The anxieties this caused have encouraged the creation of a monstrous other – a gay-liberal conspiracy – in a bid to externalize the threatening differences and bring a new unity. However, the cost of this strategy is high. Individuals can easily get crushed by the political conflicts raging around them. This has clearly been the case for high-profile figures scapegoated for their unwillingness to entirely follow a party line, who seemed to suggest the possibility of some sort of middle ground. It has also been the case for a significantly greater number of less high-profile people, particularly gay Christians, who have essentially become pawns in a political struggle. When the need to acknowledge and guard against the reality of homophobia in church circles is downplayed or denied (as it has been in conservative evangelical rhetoric) it is these people who end up bearing the cost.

It is clear now that the fracture lines between conservatives and progressives run through the middle of evangelical groupings as well as between evangelicals and liberals. As the Church of England moves towards some sort of settlement on sexuality, progressives are openly challenging the certainties of the biblical interpretation behind the consensus position, while conservatives are doubling down on the claim that scripture is clear, avoiding debate on contentious passages, and focusing more on strategies for negotiating some sort of split. Division and breakdown of community seems inevitable. However, the moment of crisis when those locked in conflict see each other as irreconcilably different is also the moment when to outside observers they seem almost identical. As in the parable of the prodigal son, it is the moment when the older son refuses to accept the return of a rebellious brother he sees as utterly unlike him that it becomes apparent exactly how far he has himself travelled away from following the example of his father. The irony of the parable is that both sons are rebellious. A crisis, bringing all the issues out into the open, can be the basis for a deeper understanding and reconciliation. It is when the older brother expresses his resentment that the father then seeks him out with the offer of reconciliation just as he had with his brother. Apocalypse is not the only possible outcome. There are signs that conservatives are still open to new perspectives, as is shown by the new prominence being given to gay voices that are critical of the church's homophobic tendencies.

My intention in this chapter has been to uncover some of the dynamics that drive the current conflict over sexuality, to reveal the complexity behind it, and to demonstrate why it is proving so impossible to 'get over'. The sexuality debate is far more complex than either side's simple 'solution' (either agreeing to maintain the consensus position and moving on or accepting same-sex relationships as equivalent to opposite sex ones) allows. In many ways it is no longer really a debate about sexuality at all. The dynamics of scandalized communities in crisis have encouraged multiple different debates to become consolidated into this one. At the acknowledged risk of over-simplification, then, I want to suggest that the sexuality debate as it is now being debated is not really about sexuality. Instead it is a proxy war being fought between different approaches to living the Christian life in the modern world. Ultimately, it is about what it means to do church and to be a Christian disciple in the modern world. To understand why sexuality might have become the key battleground for this sort of conflict requires some exploration of what modernity actually is, and why living in modernity is regarded as posing a challenge for evangelicals.

Notes

1 The roots of this pattern of exegesis in Barth is very clear, albeit unacknowledged, Karl Barth, *Church Dogmatics*, III/1, London: T&T Clark International, p. 322.

2 See also Paul, Ian, 2014, *Same Sex Unions*, Cambridge: Grove Books, p. 29, where he is more careful to state that this is the view of 'some prominent commentators', rather than being accepted by all scholars.

3 Stott, John, 1984, *Issues Facing Christians Today*, London: Harper Collins, p. xi.

4 NatCen Research, 2013, BSA 30, https://www.bsa.natcen.ac.uk/latest-report/british-social-attitudes-30/personal-relationships/homosexuality.aspx (accessed 13.2.2023).

5 Bray, Gerald, 1993, 'Editorial', *The Churchman*, 107, no. 4.

6 White, John, 1993, *Eros Redeemed: Breaking the Stranglehold of Sexual Sin*, p. 18.

7 Schmidt, Thomas E., 1995, *Straight and Narrow?*, Westmont, IL: InterVarsity Press, p. 108.

8 Schmidt, 1995, p. 130.

9 Schmidt, 1995, p. 115.

10 Stott, 1999, *New Issues Facing Christians Today*, 3rd edn, London: Marshall Pickering, pp. 402–3.

11 Stott, 1999, p. 413.

12 Stott, 1999, p. 397.

13 Evangelical Alliance, 1998, *Faith Hope Homosexuality*, p. 2.

14 Stott, 1999, p. 395. Stott's generous refusal to cast doubt on Vasey's sincerity or evangelical credentials here is notable.

15 Linzey, Andrew and Kirker, Richard, eds, 2005, *Gays and the Future of Anglicanism*, Ropley: O Books, pp. xix–xxiv.

16 Hill, Symon, 2011, 'Christianity and Homophobia in Britain Today', text of address to Camden LGBT Forum's *The Globalisation of Homosexuality* event, May 2011, http://www.ekklesia.co.uk/node/14787 (accessed 13.2.2023).

17 Stott, John and McCloughry, Roy, 2006, *Issues Facing Christians Today*, 4th edn, p. 466.

18 Reform, Letters, *Sunday Times*, November 28, 2004.

19 Gumbel, Nicky, 1995, *Searching Issues*, Eastbourne: Kingsway, p. 82.

20 Bates, Stephen, 2004, *A Church at War*, London: I.B. Tauris, p. 92.

21 Nolland, Lisa, et al. eds, 2008, *God, Gays and the Church*, London: Latimer Trust, p. 182.

22 Harrison, Glynn, 2016, *A Better Story*, Westmont, IL: InterVarsity Press, p. 184.

4

Evangelicals talking about modernity: The question behind the question

In Chapter 3 I suggested that evangelical conflict over sexuality is not really about sexuality, but about far deeper divisions over responses to modernity. The real question at stake here is nothing less than what it means to be church and do Christian discipleship in the modern world. A similar point is made by the evangelical scholar Carl Trueman, whose work we will be examining in this chapter. In his *The Rise and Triumph of the Modern Self*, an examination of modernity (which he defines in Charles Taylor's terms as 'expressive individualism') he argues:

> The sexual revolution is simply one manifestation of the larger revolution of the self that has taken place in the West. And it is only as we come to understand that wider context that we can truly understand the dynamics of the sexual politics that now dominate our culture.[1]

Although as will become apparent I disagree with some aspects of his analysis, two key insights shape both our approaches – the first is set out in the above quotation: conflict over sexuality is symptomatic of a far larger and deeper conflict within both church and society about how to respond to modernity. The second is implicit within it, but deserves stating more clearly: we are all responding to the various movements and ideas that make up modernity as natives of modernity rather than as outside observers of it. Or, as Trueman puts it: 'expressive individualism is something that affects us all. It is the very essence of the culture of which we are all a part. To put it bluntly: we are all expressive individuals now.'[2] It's important to stress this point because as we have seen, simplistic analyses of the sexuality debate tend to revolve around characterizations of progressives as modern and conservatives as pre-modern traditionalists. As will become apparent, even Trueman is not always consistent in the way he discusses this. With these two ideas in mind, the question we are exploring in this chapter can best be framed in this way: what is happening to the church in modernity that is manifesting itself in conflicts over sexuality, if everyone on both sides of the conflict is a native of modernity? My answer to this question takes me in a rather different direction from Trueman, but to explain why, I need to place his book in a wider tradition of evangelical writing about modernity.

The issue at stake here is that conservative evangelicals have generally found Trueman's second point, that we are all inescapably modern, hard to accept. The characteristic evangelical outlook on modernity has been to assume that the church is or should be somehow outside surrounding culture as a whole, shaped only by the gospel. Being shaped by surrounding culture and understanding our faith in terms of its values is to become worldly. This tendency to conceptualize church and culture as logically separable, suggesting the existence of a place outside culture where the church can stand and make decisions about the degree it wants to accept or reject aspects of culture is influenced by H. Richard Niebuhr's *Christ and Culture* (1951), which set out a typology of differing theological understandings of the relationship between the two.[3] Although Niebuhr himself is concerned to speak of 'Christ' and 'culture', the analysis he offers has often been assumed to speak of 'church' and 'world'. So in Stott's *Issues Facing Christians Today* (1984) he urges evangelicals to engage in social action in these terms (easily identifiable as Niebuhr's 'Christ against culture' and 'Christ of culture' paradigms):

> Sometimes, in a right emphasis on its 'holiness', the church has wrongly withdrawn from the world and become insulated

from it. At other times, in a right emphasis on its 'worldliness' (i.e. its immersion in the life of the world), the church has wrongly become assimilated to the world's standards and values, and so become contaminated by them.[4]

As we shall see, Stott's understanding is actually more sophisticated than this might imply – including an awareness that we cannot easily step outside our own culture to judge the degree to which we should be influenced by it. However, the prevalence of a church/world distinction among evangelicals discourages awareness of Trueman's point that 'we are all expressive individuals now'.

This tendency to conceptualize 'church' and 'world' as logically separable and to treat 'world' as synonymous with 'modernity' and 'church' as synonymous with 'gospel' has led to two common misconceptions within evangelicalism about the relationship between the church and culture. First, it encourages an identification of significant movements of cultural change in the world (particularly revolutionary ones that can plausibly be understood as dismantling the inheritance of Christendom), as inevitably representing a rejection of the gospel. Second, it encourages a blindness to the degree to which the church itself is always and inevitably shaped by the worldly culture of its members. For obvious reasons, the two misconceptions go hand in glove – the more surrounding culture is seen to represent rejection of the gospel the harder it is to recognize the degree to which the church's own life and understanding of the gospel is inevitably an expression of that same culture. The fact is that, although we can develop a distinct church subculture that is different from and critical of the cultural mainstream, it will inevitably still be a subculture of modernity. A necessary spiritual distancing from the values and practices of modernity will actually manifest itself as a distinctive set of modern values and modern practices held by the modern members of the modern church who have never at any point ceased to be modern people living in a modern world.

In this chapter I explore the degree to which an understanding of modernity as monstrous, spiritually dangerous and implacably opposed to the gospel has become a dominant narrative within conservative evangelicalism. In Stott's terms they see worldliness as the greatest danger. This allies them with traditional Catholics, who hold a similar view, and sets them on a collision course with liberals and progressive evangelicals who self-consciously align themselves with modernity (who see Stott's 'purist form of holiness' as the greatest danger). This amounts to a significant realignment of Anglican identities, producing deep divisions within evangelicalism which manifest in the conviction that faithfulness to the gospel is at stake.

My argument within this chapter is that this is actually what the sexuality debate is about, and this is the ultimate reason why the conviction that it is a first order of faith is so widespread. Within this framework of understanding conservatives see a progressive stance as assimilation to the world and therefore unfaithfulness to the unchanging gospel. Progressives, in the same framework, see conservatives as withdrawing from the world Christ died for and disowning the gospel imperative of love for the world. It is all too easy for evangelicals on both sides to see the other as false teachers and syncretists. This is the wider backdrop in which debates about sexuality take place, the real reason why sexuality is regarded as a first order issue of faith, and failure to recognize that this prevents meaningful dialogue from occurring.

Part I – Resisting modernity as a first order issue

Dystopian evangelical visions of modernity

We have already noted in Chapter 3 that the link of modernity to permissiveness, understood as evidence of the dark spiritual times we live in, became a mainstay of some conservative evangelical writing in the Nineties, linking the spiritual warfare emphasis of the charismatic movement to the culture wars of conservatives. However, this understanding of modernity as departure from the truth of the gospel and a societal wrong-turn leading inevitably to the decline of the Christian West is far more than an affectation of some writers in the Nineties. The idea that the Sixties represent a turning away from godliness can be traced back to the evangelical Os Guinness's *The Dust of Death* (1973), which comprehensively analysed the spiritual and intellectual failings of the modern West:

> This is the West of our time. The loss of centre can no longer be disguised. The infinite polarizations are only illustrative features of this disintegration. The striptease of humanism and the abortion of the counter culture should now be accepted as facts germane to any discussion of the future direction of our society.[5]

For Guinness, a revival of Christianity was the only hope for a failing Western civilization. There are obvious links between this analysis and the culture wars of the US, as set out in James Davison Hunter's study *Culture Wars* (1991). Hunter demonstrated that a conservative evangelical analysis of modernity as turning away from God is at the heart of the development of the Religious Right, who have idealized a pre-Sixties past and demonized the permissive society:

> So warns Pat Robertson: 'Either we will return to the moral integrity and original dreams of the founders of this nation … or we will give ourselves over more and more to hedonism, to all forms of destructive anti-social behaviour, to political apathy, and ultimately to the forces of anarchy and disintegration.'[6]

The interweaving of evangelicalism with conservative political views in the US has attracted considerable analysis, particularly since white evangelicals became prominent among the supporters of Donald Trump. However, it is important to recognize that the dystopian view of modernity identifiable in some strands of evangelicalism was not originally a political outlook even if, as

Hunter has identified, it swiftly became co-opted for political ends. Its origins are in an assessment of the modern West that is primarily spiritual and apologetic. Guinness was himself a student of Francis Schaeffer, founder of the L'Abri community in Switzerland, whose three key books (written in the Sixties and Seventies) were republished in a single accessible paperback by Crossway (in the US) and InterVarsity Press (in the UK) in the Nineties. Schaeffer was fundamentally an apologist, who developed a distinctive methodology for evangelistic engagement. Influenced by the Dutch Neo-Calvinist Cornelius Van Til, Schaeffer was convinced that Christians and non-Christians have worldviews that are ultimately irreconcilable, because they are based on utterly different presuppositions. However, both are rational and inhabit the same created universe, which is only truly explicable by reference to the Christian worldview. Therefore the non-Christian is always ultimately espousing a worldview that cannot make rational sense of the created universe in which they live: 'in fact, no non-Christian can be consistent to the logic of his own presuppositions ... As Christianity is the truth of what is there, to deny this, on the basis of another system, is to stray from the real world.'[7]

On this basis Schaeffer engaged with significant modern philosophies to demonstrate the way in which they were ultimately futile attempts to rationalize life without reference to God. He pioneered an apologetic technique called 'taking the roof off', which involved identifying the point where the non-Christian knew something to be true for which their worldview could provide no rational explanation, and removing the conceptual 'roof' that provides shelter from reality, exposing the inadequacy of their beliefs and creating an opening for the gospel. This basic approach became highly influential among evangelicals. For our purposes there are two key implications of Schaeffer's approach for the development of evangelical views on modernity: first, modernity is understood as being primarily a non-Christian system of thought, a 'worldview', and one that is inherently flawed and necessarily different from a biblical worldview. Successful evangelism comes from confident engagement with those holding to this worldview in the certainty that their beliefs do not explain the reality of the world in which they live. Second, evangelicals are understood as holding to an unchanging biblical worldview that is rooted in truth, and which is utterly irreconcilable with modernity:

> There are certain unchangeable facts which are true. These have no relationship to the shifting tides. They make the Christian system what it is, and if they are altered, Christianity becomes something else ... If we do this we are no longer communicating Christianity, and what we have left is no different than the surrounding consensus.[8]

This basic outlook has been foundational for some strands of modern evangelicalism, particularly in America. Philosophical analysis of modernity as a hostile environment, often with an apologetic aim, has become a recognizable genre in evangelical writing over the last 60 years. Don Carson's *The Gagging of God* (1996) further developed this tradition. Carson, drawing on the analysis of Hunter and Guinness, described modernity in terms of pluralism. This is understood both in the literal sense that it contains multiple communities and perspectives, and in the far deeper sense of the intellectual belief that truth itself is plural, lacking in absolutes. It is this philosophical form of pluralism, understood as the ideology of modernity, that Carson identifies as an abandonment of the truth of the gospel. Western culture has turned away from the godly virtues of the past:

> This vision of things has largely been replaced by what they call the therapeutic model. Feelings and emotions assume extraordinary importance; individualistic self-fulfilment becomes the prime good. And often this self-fulfilment will be achieved, it is thought, by self-expression. What was formerly considered to be cheerful self-discipline and self-control is now dismissed with contempt as dangerous repression.[9]

Carson argued that this outlook was the basic philosophy of Western culture as a whole, and represented a wholesale rejection of Christian values that would lead to the collapse of society.

This evaluation of modernity as a dystopia that is fundamentally antithetical to the gospel and objectively leading to societal collapse has therefore been a consistent thread in evangelical writing from the Sixties. In Britain in particular it has been bolstered by a growing awareness of the decline in church attendance that has occurred over this period. In the Fifties around a third of the adult population in Britain could be counted as at least fringe members and occasional attenders at church. By the end of the twentieth century this had reduced to a small fraction of the number – with the 'fringe' becoming ever more irregular in attendance and ever less likely to claim even a nominal Christian identity, and the number of regular attenders being very small indeed.[10] The cultural gap between the churchgoing and non-churchgoing sections of the population (highlighted by the pressure to allow Sunday trading) helped to reinforce the sense of modernity as antithetical to the gospel. Increasingly references to church and Christianity in popular culture became sparse and either comical or negative.

The fact that within a picture of overall decline it is noticeable that liberal churches have declined faster than more conservative ones has meant that it has also become commonplace for evangelicals to link liberal theological 'compromise with the world' with church decline (notwithstanding the fact that evangelical churches have also declined).[11] This sort of analysis that modernity is inimicable to faith and, if you accommodate it, it will destroy you has drawn some support from the sociological analysis of James Davidson Hunter. Hunter undertook a study of evangelical churches in the US, arguing that modernity is a hostile environment for religious worldviews, requiring evangelicalism (and every individual evangelical) to engage in a kind of bargaining process with modernity in order to survive. This results in a kind of horse trading, where the demands of modernity are accommodated in some places (an emphasis on individualism and acceptance of consumerism, for example) in order to be resisted elsewhere (sexual morality). In Hunter's view, evangelicals are ultimately doomed – they can hold on to some sites of resistance by tactically withdrawing from others, but they can't change the final outcome. Hunter's thesis has been challenged by the later work of Christian Smith, whose observation that by resisting modernity in places and accommodating it in others evangelicals are actually flourishing has been welcomed by some evangelicals. However, it is noticeable that it is Hunter's evaluation of modernity as corrosive to faith that has had the biggest impact on evangelical self-understanding.

It is this history of dystopian visions of modernity which forms the backdrop to Trueman's *The Rise and Triumph of the Modern Self*. It is important to recognize that, as I have already pointed out, this is a far more sophisticated analysis than that offered by Schaeffer, Guinness or Carson. Trueman's analysis of modernity focuses on the way in which advances in technology have interacted with a set of philosophical traditions to create an unprecedented cultural shift in the West. He draws on the work of three key figures in this: the sociologist Philip Rieff, the philosopher Charles Taylor, and the ethicist Alasdair MacIntyre. It is clear that of the three it is Rieff's theories and concepts that form the heart of Trueman's analysis, with Taylor and MacIntyre being drawn in at discrete moments to supplement this. Rieff argues that the development of modernity is a decisive shift of era. Throughout human history, societies have functioned as either what he terms first or second world societies, in which the ultimate authority or justification for morality, culture and all the institutions of society derive from a sacred order. In first world (or pagan) societies this takes the form of a mythological framework for the world. In second world (or Christendom) societies this takes the form of a religious faith. Modernity, however, is a third world society that does not look to a sacred order as the justification for its moral codes and institutions. Instead, this justification is found in each individual person living authentically. Rieff describes this as the triumph of the therapeutic – where the attitude encouraged through psychotherapy is universalized as the correct way of life for all. The individual must free themselves of all that represses them to be their true selves. All activities, institutions and moral codes are now re-evaluated from this perspective. Our inner lives have become the source of all authority, and there is no sense of an external objective truth that might rightly constrain us, our sense of identity is now plastic, or malleable, able to be reshaped as we choose. Any external authority or institution that prevents us from being our true selves is understood to be oppressive and to be dismantled. Trueman extensively documents the philosophical tradition that has led to this, taking in Freud, Marxist and feminist thinkers, and linking these to earlier traditions of thought and to wider expressions of this in art, politics and education. His argument is that modernity is a deeply rooted philosophical movement within Western culture that is shared by the majority of the population who have absorbed these ideas without even being aware of their origin.

It is central to Rieff's analysis, and thus central to Trueman's (though not to Taylor's), that these developments are catastrophic and represent the inevitable decline and collapse of Western society. Trueman adopts Rieff's terminology in describing modernity as an anticulture, an inherently destabilizing and nihilistic society that will destroy all that went before it and then itself. Those cultural impulses and trends that facilitate the advance of the anticulture are therefore rightly termed 'deathworks':

> The intellectual class is devoted ... to the subversion, destabilization, and destruction of the [preceding] culture's traditions ... They are, in the words of Rieff, creating not a culture but an anticulture, called such because of its iconoclastic, purely destructive attitude toward all that the first and second worlds hold dear.[12]

It is inherent to this conceptualization of the cultural shift now occurring that modernity is effectively irredeemable. It represents a cultural wrong turn into a deathly void. There can therefore be no common ground and no reconciliation between inhabitants of a second and third world, nor can any healthy community or culture be built on the foundation of a third world.

It is at this point that certain unresolved tensions become apparent in Trueman's work. He on the one hand asserts strongly that we are all expressive individuals now, all natives of modernity, while at the same time asserting that to be a native of modernity is to live in a third world that is utterly irredeemable. He treats Rieff's third world 'therapeutic man' as equivalent to Taylor's modern 'expressive individual' which as we have seen he argues we all undeniably are, yet sees the therapeutic man as a tainted product of anticulture. Where exactly the modern church sits in relation to the third world is therefore never entirely clear. Is the church therefore also necessarily part of the anticulture, or is it somehow immune to such cultural shifts in the outside world? The closest Trueman comes to resolving this is in the suggestion that second and third worlds currently co-exist, locked in conflict, implying that the church might logically be seen as a second world island within a third world sea:

> The conflict between traditional religion and modern sexual identities is a clash – perhaps the quintessential clash – between the second-world culture and the anticulture of the third, so completely opposed are they at the most fundamental level. There is no compromise that can really be reached here because there is no way that the one can be assimilated to the other. They rest on completely different premises and are aimed at antithetical outcomes.[13]

This evaluation is, of course, very similar to Schaeffer's. Christian and non-Christian worldviews are irreconcilable. Trueman also shows Carson's characteristic emphasis on the need to guard against syncretism and the unthinking adoption of anticulture values and practices within the church. As Trueman can readily be aligned with this wider tradition of evangelical dystopian accounts of modernity it therefore seems likely that despite the ambiguities of his discussion, Trueman's interpretation of modernity will be assimilated to a dystopian vision and his hints that the relationship between church and culture may be more complex will be ignored. Read this way, Trueman's analysis effectively supercharges the monstrous vision of modernity that is common among conservative evangelicals. Modernity now represents the complete collapse of society in the West, a cultural wrong turn into an anticulture with which there can be no dialogue, and that the church must constantly guard against infiltrating its own community. Mission, properly understood, therefore involves pulling people out of a toxic wasteland into safety, and will necessarily involve a careful decontamination process to guard against deathworks. Trueman's own closing remarks, advising churches to guard against the encroachment of aesthetic-based logic, his suggestion that the church as a community can be an alternative to expressive individualism, and his warning that Christian sexual morality must not be abandoned, all suggest a vision of the church as a second-world enclave in modernity.[14]

However, it is important to recognize that the relationship between church and modernity remains an unresolved tension in Trueman's work, even if conservative evangelicals are likely to immediately collapse this tension in co-opting him. Trueman continues to insist that we are all expressive individualist Christians now, and yet obviously believes that this foundational assimilation by modernity does not mean that the church has already finally collapsed into an anticulture. How this could be the case is not something Trueman chooses to explore, but he does give a few hints as to how the tension between the two might be resolved, primarily by toning down some of Rieff's dystopian emphases. In tracing the history of individualism, he corrects Rieff, pointing out that the idea that the individual's inner world is the key to understanding truth, far from being a modern anticultural influence, has its origins in Christianity.[15] Expressive individualism is the heir of Paul, Augustine and Luther. He also at one point argues that expressive individualism is not entirely irredeemable and in fact could be seen to be an improvement on pre-modern culture:

> Expressive individualism is not an unmitigated evil. In some ways, it marks a significant improvement on that which it replaced. One of the aspects of the modern culture of expressive individualism is the emphasis it places on the inherent dignity of the individual ... And that is something with which Christians should sympathize ... the problem with expressive individualism ... is the fact that expressive individualism has detached these concepts of individual dignity and value from any kind of grounding in a sacred order.[16]

There is therefore clearly a strand of Trueman's thinking that recognizes that, despite the Rieffian language of anticulture and deathworks, modernity and Christianity (and protestantism in particular) have a shared history, common impulses, and far more common ground than he elsewhere acknowledges.

Monstrous modernity and the sexuality debate

We will return to explore this unresolved tension in Trueman's thought later, but for now it is important to examine more closely some of the ways in which conservative evangelicals have woven together this dystopian understanding of modernity with their discussion of sexuality. Trueman himself makes this connection explicitly, using the trans debate as a key example throughout (in which it is clear that he sees the progressive outlook as a dangerous and nonsensical deathwork), and exploring queer theory as a key contributor to the philosophy of modernity. The merging of the two strands of conservative evangelical writing (on sexuality and on modernity) is shown at its clearest, however, in Harrison's *A Better Story* (2016). The bulk of the book constitutes an analysis of modernity along the lines set out by Schaeffer, Carson and Trueman. Sexuality is explored as a point of tension between the Christian and non-Christian worldviews in Schaeffer's terms – this is the place where the worldview of modernity fails to explain reality, and can therefore be used as a way in for the gospel. Harrison sees progressive understandings as deathworks, having their roots in 'radical new forms of individualism' engaged in a 'bid for freedom from all authority and tradition'.[17] On this basis, he argues that the correct response to the sexuality debate is therefore *not* to present a biblical and ethical argument, engaging with opposing arguments as if they had validity. As Trueman argues, this is pointless – there is no common ground, the worldviews are irreconcilable. Rather, Harrison follows Schaeffer's apologetic approach. He confidently asserts the Christian understanding, resisting any pressure to change the unchanging truth, in the certainty that it is the Christian worldview that best explains reality – it is a better story:

> We cannot forget that this is a clash of moral vision: we can't prevent those with different concepts of goodness and flourishing from finding offence, danger even, in what we profess. But for the life of the world, for the sake of the gospel, we cannot remain silent.[18]

This is ethics done as apologetics – with the aim being not to convince but to convert the listener. By implication then, this is an approach to the sexuality debate that assumes those who disagree with the consensus position are outside the faith, in the grip of the anticulture (or, in Harrison's terms holding to a form of gnosticism), and in need of conversion.

Under the controlling influence of an understanding of modernity as monstrous there is no possibility of genuine dialogue, and attempting to enter into one simply opens one up to the dangerous influence of the anticulture. The only possible response is to seek the conversion of the one with whom you find yourself in disagreement. The understanding that modernity itself is monstrous underlies all convictions that sexuality is a first order issue. If the sexuality debate is approached as the quintessential example of the confrontation between the gospel and the world (as Trueman suggests), then it is axiomatic that it constitutes a first order issue. This is why there is agreement between conservative evangelicals that the sexuality debate constitutes a first order issue of faith and yet they seem unconcerned that they do not agree on the reasons why: the authority of clearly interpreted scripture, a doctrinal understanding of gendered human nature, or the Christian tradition of heterosexual marriage. It is none of these and all of them. All are in some way symptomatic of the clash between gospel and world that the anticulture represents. None of the specifics of the sexuality debate are the reason why it constitutes a first order issue, it is simply the fact that it is exemplary of the need not to compromise with modernity.

Part II – Defusing the debate

Resolving the tensions in Trueman's analysis

In the first part of our discussion, we have explored how conservative evangelicals have come to adopt an understanding of modernity itself as monstrous. This means that any issue (sexuality and trans issues are the two specifically highlighted by Trueman) that can be identified as symbolic of the encroachment of modernity instantly becomes a first order issue. It is a deathwork, the acceptance of which by the church represents faithlessness to the gospel. Genuine dialogue over these issues is impossible, because you are effectively engaging in debate with those you see as already outside the church, and the appropriate response is to seek their conversion.

Defusing the sexuality debate necessarily involves dismantling this monstrous vision of modernity that makes genuine dialogue impossible, and compromise a betrayal of the gospel. In this second part of our discussion I therefore want to explore the possibility of an alternative and non-monstrous evaluation of modernity for evangelicals, which might enable a humbler and less defended conversation.

DEFUSING THE SEXUALITY DEBATE

I suggested earlier that Trueman's analysis, which represents the most sophisticated conservative evangelical evaluation of modernity to date, actually contains more nuance and ambiguity than might be recognized, not least due to his engagement with Taylor and MacIntyre, neither of whom would uncritically support Rieff's dystopian vision of modernity as anticulture. However, the insights of Taylor and MacIntyre are not fully integrated into Trueman's argument, creating unresolved tensions within it. In Trueman's understanding, Rieff's thesis of the emergence of the anticulture is allowed to dominate, which means that the characteristic emphases of Taylor and MacIntyre are significantly muffled. Allowing their approaches more space to counterbalance Rieff would go some way to creating a more balanced and less dystopian view of modernity.

In contrast to Rieff's monstrous vision of modernity as an anticulture that is implacably and uniformly hostile to Christianity, Taylor stresses the degree to which modernity is multifaceted, and even its overtly secular manifestations do not seem to entail the complete erasure of Christianity:

> The present fractured expressivist culture ... seems very inhospitable to belief ... and yet the sense that there is something more presses in. Great numbers of people feel it ... and quite wildly and unpredictably. Our age is very far from settling into a comfortable unbelief ... Such are the strange and complex conditions of belief in our age.[19]

For Taylor, therefore, the thing that requires explanation in modernity is not so much the way in which faith and ultimate values become hard to justify, but the indisputable fact that despite and in the midst of this they continue to emerge.

In fact his difference from Trueman goes deeper than this. Taylor goes out of his way to critique the sort of identification of Christian faith with functional Western society that Trueman, building on Rieff, is making. The argument that modernity, in distancing itself from Christianity and Christian beliefs and values, is becoming an anticulture rests on the assumption that

Christendom is an ideal we depart from at our peril. Taylor is wary of this assumption:

> There has been a long-standing tendency in the West to slide towards an identification of Christian faith and civilizational order. This not only makes us lose sight of the full transformation that Christians are called to, but it also makes us lose a crucial critical distance from the order that we identify as Christendom, whether it be the one at present established, or some earlier one that we are fighting to restore.[20]

Taylor argues the case for Christianity to maintain a critical distance from the interests of the social order, arguing against both those who adopt an uncritical vision of progress and those who yearn to restore a past paradigm (naming particularly those like the Religious Right who think pre-Sixties America got it right and we have to repudiate whatever deviates from that standard).[21]

Taylor therefore has little interest in supporting the argument that it is impossible to live the life of faith within modernity. Indeed, he takes it as axiomatic that we have no alternative option to living the life of faith within it. It is the only way any of us have ever known to live the life of faith. Expressive individualism, we might say, doesn't care if you think you are an expressive individual or not, though it might allow itself an ironic chuckle at those expressive individuals who don't. Trueman says we are all expressive individuals now, but he does not follow the logic of this statement through, treating it as some sort of constant temptation to compromise ourselves with modernity, rather than being an unavoidable fact of our existence. Taylor's point is that living the life of faith in modernity is precisely what we are called to do, avoiding the temptation to yearn to restore a golden age of Christianity.

Trueman makes use of MacIntyre primarily to draw on his argument that modernity has made conventional appeals to an objective set of externally validated moral values rooted in institutions or philosophy no longer viable, reducing much of our moral discourse to emotivism. However, this observation is just the starting point of MacIntyre's argument. He argues that this should prompt us to reconsider the way we approach ethics and in particular to revisit the possibilities of understanding ethics as making sense primarily within a community in which we come to know who we are in dialogue with others: 'the self has to find its moral identity in and through its membership in communities such as those of the family, the neighbourhood, the city and the tribe'.[22] Unlike Trueman, MacIntyre does not conclude that the prevalence of emotivism in moral discourse suggests that the concept of right and wrong has now been irretrievably lost and reduced to expressions of individual preference under the influence of an anticulture. Instead he suggests that within modernity it is possible to recover a different approach where our moral values are primarily formed in conversation and in community, as part of a tradition with a history: 'a living tradition then is an historically extended, socially embodied argument, and an argument precisely in part about the goods that constitute that tradition'.[23] So rather than Trueman's vision of a third world as an ahistorical moral wasteland with no clear sense of right and wrong, MacIntyre suggests that it is perfectly possible for traditions of moral and practical reasoning to flourish within modernity: 'It is indeed a feature of all those traditions with whose histories we have been specifically concerned that in one way or another all of them have survived so as to become not only possible, but actual, forms of practical life within the domain of modernity.'[24] Although Trueman makes a gesture towards accepting MacIntyre's argument in stressing the need for the church to retain a grip on its own history and to invest in being a community, he shows little sign of recognizing that the sort of historically informed neo-Aristotelean community envisaged by MacIntyre would function very differently from a typical evangelical church. Rather, he suggests that the church must fight against the anticulture to keep the possibility of history and community alive.

If these insights of Taylor and MacIntyre are allowed their proper weight, they start to address some of the tensions we earlier identified in Trueman's analysis of modernity. A modernity that all of us are inescapably part of, and that has not and cannot erase the necessity of the moral and the spiritual, must necessarily be one in which the life of faith we are all engaged in is possible. A modernity in which communities embed their history in powerful narratives and nurture virtues in their members is not one where church can only exist and thrive by restoring a lost golden age, or relentlessly resisting the forces of modernity. On this basis, we can curb some of the excesses of Rieff's analysis, refusing the catastrophism that dismisses modernity as an irredeemable anticulture. This does not mean denying that many of the ideas and impulses of modernity are antithetical to the gospel. A critical distance should be maintained. However, as Taylor notes, the church should also resist the temptation of a return to a golden age – which may involve admitting that many of the ideas and impulses of pre-modernity were likewise antithetical to the gospel (and yet somehow the gospel and the church survived to dance on their graves). As Trueman concedes, modernity is in some respects a genuine improvement on what went before (and we might include the modern repudiation of homophobia as one of these areas).

A non-monstrous modernity

If we are to develop a more balanced understanding of modernity than that set out by Trueman, a good place to start might be the suggestive hint he makes, drawing on Taylor, that expressive individualism can be seen to trace its origins back to Christianity, and in particular to protestantism:

> Charles Taylor and others have argued at great length that the Reformation was the watershed that unleashed the notion of religious choice in the West and therefore laid the foundations for the rise of the expressive individual as the normative self.[25]

The implications of this for evangelicals, who trace their heritage to the Reformation, are significant. It suggests that evangelicals, far from being a holdover of a pre-modern second world, are in fact natives of the emerging third world. They are a movement of expressive individualism, sprung from exactly the same tradition of thought that led to the triumph of the therapeutic. This, although disturbing for those holding to a monstrous vision of modernity, is actually reflective of fairly mainstream historical understanding. David Bebbington, the historian of evangelicalism, is clear that evangelicals emerged as children of the Enlightenment, and argues that evangelicalism is characterized by nothing more than its ability to adapt to rapidly changing cultural surroundings.[26]

The historian Tom Holland goes further in his recent *Dominion: The Making of the Western Mind*. Holland's argument is essentially that modernity itself is thoroughly Christian, to the extent that it is impossible to explain its development except by reference to Christianity. In fact, Holland's entire line of argument systematically undermines Trueman's supposition that the triumph of the therapeutic, the rise of expressive individualism, and the politicization of the sexual represents a rejection of the gospel or Christian morality. On the contrary, Holland suggests it is the gospel that has made these things possible. In describing the current 'woke' era of the West, he argues:

> The retreat of Christian belief did not seem to imply any necessary retreat of Christian values. Quite the contrary... the trace elements of Christianity continued to infuse people's morals and presumptions so utterly that many failed even to detect their presence ... Had it been otherwise, then no one would ever have got woke.[27]

All of this suggests a need for rather more nuance in understanding the nature of modernity and its relationship with Christianity, even (and perhaps especially), at those points where it might seem to be functioning as a destructive anti-culture. Trueman has highlighted the extent to which the cultural iconoclasm of modernity, its 'wokeness', represents a destructive and anti-Christian impulse. However, Holland suggests that it is at this point that modernity reveals most strongly its Christian heritage. In Holland's terms, it represents profoundly Christian impulses and values divorced from their roots in Christian worship and in some cases turned against the church itself. As we have seen, Trueman himself acknowledges one of the basic impulses of modernity is concern for the dignity of the individual which is problematic only because divorced from the sacred order. 'Wokeness' can therefore plausibly be understood as Christian concern for the dignity of the individual turned against the very Christian traditions, institutions and practices that have historically nurtured that concern. Once described in this way, the 'family resemblance' between modernity and the Reformation becomes obvious. From this perspective, both represent critique of a particular manifestation of Christianity on the basis of fundamentally Christian values. With this in mind, it is worth revisiting the contrast Trueman attempts to draw between the sort of cultural iconoclasm seen in modernity and that of the Reformation.

Recognizing some similarities between modernity and the Reformation as expressions of cultural iconoclasm, Trueman argues that the Reformation is best understood as a conflict within a second world over the implications of sacred order, not a third world repudiation of that sacred order:

> Protestant elites were not committed so much to cultural iconoclasm as to what they considered to be cultural retrieval ... one of the hallmarks of this reality is that the Bible as a sacred text lay at the heart of the sixteenth-century church reforms for both sides of the Reformation debate.[28]

A moment's reflection suggests that although this may be apparent to us as disinterested observers from several centuries distance, it was far from apparent at the time (and might still be disputed by some Roman Catholics now). The question of whether adherence to the Bible alone as sacred text was enough to ensure sacred order was upheld was precisely the dispute at the heart of the Reformation. Protestants believed it was, and Catholics believed it wasn't. If, as Trueman suggests, the difference between a creative cultural impulse and a destructive anticultural impulse genuinely rests on such fine distinctions, the necessary corollary must be that discerning the difference between the two is not easy. Particularly if you are one of those whose traditions, institutions and patterns of behaviour are being creatively reimagined through a process of 'cultural retrieval'. Many of those who lived through the destruction of saints' shrines, the dissolution of monastaries, the removal of stone altars and the whitewashing of church walls would doubtless feel strongly what they were experiencing were the deathworks of an anticulture. How can today's conservative evangelicals be sure they are not reacting in the same way as yesterday's faithful Catholics?

The fact is that the movements that Trueman describes as involved purely in destructive cultural repudiation *do* understand themselves to be involved in acts of cultural retrieval. To pick an example at random, Susannah Cornwall's *Un/Familiar Theology: Reconceiving Sex, Reproduction and Generativity* (2017), published in T&T Clark's Rethinking Theologies series, is a discussion of the theological concepts of marriage, family, parenting and reproduction. Cornwall is self-consciously engaged in the sort of unpicking of traditional understandings that Trueman characterizes as the deathworks of an anticulture, drawing attention to marginalized voices, arguing for theology and practice to be rethought in light of the experiences of those previously excluded by them. She frequently cites the experience of the marginalized and an array of queer theologians, post-modern philosophers and artists to support her ideas. I will not here engage in any detailed discussion of her proposals, but I want to draw attention to two characteristics of her approach. The first is that Cornwall's approach is not to simply disregard all existing tradition and institutions. Rather, she draws creatively on an array of lesser-known traditional sources and neglected theological themes to critique current theologies and practices and make a case for alternatives. She describes her own intent in this way:

> From its earliest days, the Christian tradition has contained a stream that figures reproduction and generativity as more than biological, and that queries normative and hegemonic constructions of masculinity, femininity and interpersonal relationship. In this book, I suggest that patterns of bodily and gendered givenness may legitimately be reinterpreted and reframed in light of Christianity's own traditions.[29]

Now it is perfectly possible to argue that Cornwall fails to do this convincingly, or that the sort of reinterpretation she is seeking to engage in is simply not viable. However, it is hard to deny that in her own mind she is committed in Trueman's terms 'not so much to cultural iconoclasm as cultural retrieval'.

The second characteristic of her approach I wish to note is that it is self-consciously constructive. Her avowed intention is to find a theological understanding of key institutions like marriage and family that enables the church to continue to celebrate and affirm these institutions in the future. There is no triumphant desire to iconoclastically sweep away these institutions as inherently problematic and move into a future where every individual charts their own course unhindered by the restraints of moral codes, faithfulness to tradition, or familial institutions, as Trueman suggests. Rather, although the complexity of family and marriage in modernity is acknowledged, and the difficulties of valorizing only the traditional models is stressed, Cornwall is seeking to find ways to continue to celebrate these things as genuine goods by reimagining them. Again, it is in large part irrelevant if we feel Cornwall's approach is legitimate, the point I am making is simply that if, as Trueman suggests, the difference between cultural repudiation and cultural retrieval is to be found not in the perceptions of those whose culture is being demolished but in the intent of those doing the demolition, then it becomes very hard to deny that Cornwall might in fact be engaged in cultural retrieval.

All of this suggests that Trueman's confidence in being able to straightfowardly discern 'good' cultural iconoclasm from 'bad' cultural iconoclasm is misplaced. At this point it is worth bearing in mind that Trueman, writing as a conservative evangelical in 2022 at the height of a politicized debate over sexuality and gender, has a lot invested in the idea that these are first order issues and it is straightfoward to determine who is in the right and who is in the wrong. To find a more measured response to these questions, it might be helpful to look to a conservative evangelical writing at a slightly earlier period: John Stott.

Humbler discernment

In 1992, Stott published *The Contemporary Christian: An Urgent Plea for Double Listening*, a book he described as a 'companion volume' to *Issues Facing Christians Today*. The book was an attempt to address some of the underlying theological questions for Christian belief raised by the modern world. Unlike *Issues* it was not to go through multiple editions during the following decades (though after his death a slightly modernized version was published in 2019 as a multi-volume series). The book thus pre-dates some of the more combative discussions of sexuality and the hardening of a monstrous vision of modernity, and potentially throws an illuminating light on more extreme stances that have developed since.

Stott is no defender of the idea that evangelicalism is simply adherence to an unchanging pre-modern tradition. He makes the case for a modern evangelical faith, recognizing the gap between historical faith and the modern world, and arguing that simple restatement of tradition would be increasingly incomprehensible to a modern world that could not see its relevance. The course he wishes to steer is one avoiding on the one hand a retreat into the past and a literalistic adherence to scripture or, on the other an accommodation of the world that betrays the truths of the Word. Although alert to the dangers of syncretism, Stott therefore seeks to find a way to 'develop a Christian mind which is both shaped by the truths of historic, Biblical Christianity, and acquainted with the realities of the contemporary world. How can we relate the Word to the world, understanding the world in the light of the Word, and even understanding the Word in the light of the world?'[30]

Clearly, then, Stott's basic conceptualization of the church in modernity is closer to the one I have outlined above than it is to Trueman's. Stott does not see the church as engaged in a life or death struggle with an anticulture, with which genuine dialogue is impossible. The task of the church is not simply attentiveness to and preservation of biblical tradition, but also creatively working to make the gospel relevant by attentiveness to and learning from the modern world. He makes a case for an evangelicalism that frankly acknowledges that what is being asked of it is to engage sympathetically with modernity. Although acknowledging that the voice of the world is not to be listened to with the same deference given to the Word, Stott unapologetically calls evangelicals to engage in a 'double listening' that shows sympathy to both voices:

> We listen to the Word with humble reverence, anxious to understand it, and resolved to believe and obey what we come to understand. We listen to the world with critical alertness, anxious to understand it too, and resolved not necessarily to believe and obey it, but to sympathize with it and seek grace to discover how the gospel relates to it.[31]

By definition this means coming with an open mind, rather than the certainty that the old orthodoxy remains the correct response.

As a cautionary example he discusses Job's comforters:

> One only wishes that they had continued as they began, and kept their mouths shut. Instead, they trotted out their conventional orthodoxy, that every sinner suffers for his own sins, in the most unfeeling, insensitive way. They did not really listen to what Job had to say. They merely repeated

their own thoughtless and heartless claptrap, until in the end God rebuked them for not having spoken about him what was right.[32]

The issue was not that they didn't know their theology, it was that they did not listen to the reality of the situation they were confronted with, and on that basis God rebuked them for not having spoken of him what was right. The double listening that Stott commends is therefore not simply to be understood as attending to scripture and finding relevant illustrations of its truth, it is going deeper to find the genuine points of connection between modernity and the gospel, in the certainty that they are there:

> It is the faculty of listening to two voices at the same time, the voice of God through Scripture and the voices of men and women around us. These voices will often contradict one other, but our purpose in listening to them both is to discover how they relate to each other … For then we see that the adjectives 'historical' and 'contemporary' are not incompatible, we learn to apply the Word to the world, and we proclaim good news which is both true and new.[33]

It is already apparent that Stott's general approach is far more open to genuine dialogue and the finding of common ground than Trueman's. Where Trueman sees modernity as an anticulture with which there can be no meeting of minds, Stott urges the Christian to listen sympathetically with the aim of finding how the gospel relates to the modern world, in the confidence that such a meeting place is there waiting to be discovered. Although there are some similarities between Stott's attempt to find where the gospel relates to the modern world and Schaeffer's attempt to identify the point of tension between the two there is a significant and instructive difference between them. Schaeffer was attempting to find a faultline in the other's beliefs that he could use to reveal the inadequacy of their entire worldview. Schaeffer's approach does not require a sympathetic entering into the experience of the other at all. It assumes from the beginning that the Christian already knows the truth of both their own and the other's situation and has nothing to learn. Stott, however, is seeking to sit beside the other, to listen to both their experience and the gospel, and in the process to discover a truth that might be new to both of them.

In a later section entitled 'Transposing the Word', Stott turns to consider how scriptural truth can be applied to the modern world, arguing for the adoption of a practice of 'cultural transposition' of texts rather than a literalistic and culture-blind application. Stott's exact methodology here is less significant than the broad principles he sets out. His understanding of the authority of scripture and the need for interpretation is robustly evangelical and non-literalist, recognizing that the word of God is to be read reverently but with critical awareness – attending to its literary, historical, cultural and linguistic character. In his estimation however, the task of bridging the gap between our own culture and that of the biblical authors is the greatest difficulty in correctly understanding and applying scripture – requiring both imaginative correlation and a willingness to see where scripture challenges us, and he is frank that the church has frequently failed to do this well. His words on this point are relevant and challenging enough that it's worth quoting him at length:

> Church history is full of the church's cultural blind spots. How is it, I ask myself, that the Christian conscience not only approved but actually glamorized those terrible medieval crusades ... or how is it that torture could ever have been employed in the name of Jesus Christ to combat heresy and enforce orthodoxy ... Again, how is it that the cruel degradations of slavery and the slave trade were not abolished in the so-called Christian West until 1800 years after Christ? Or how is it that racial prejudice and environmental pollution have become widely recognized as the evils they are only since the Second World War? Such is the catalogue of some of the worst blind spots, which have marred the church's testimony

down the ages. None of them can be defended from Scripture, although tortuous attempts have been made to do so. All are due rather to a misreading of Scripture or an unwillingness to sit under its authority. God's people were blinded by tradition. They had other agendas; they were not in a mind or mood to listen to God.[34]

From his discussion in *Issues* it is clear that Stott would be happy to add homophobia to this list of the church's cultural blind spots – all examples of occasions when the church has been unable to recognize that its own theology, tradition and practices are based on misreadings of scripture. Significantly for our purposes it is also clear from Stott's words that he frankly acknowledges that it is only with the advent of modernity that some of these blind spots have become apparent. Implicitly then, Stott's discussion suggests that far from being a period in which the West has drifted ever further from the truth of the gospel expressed in Christian tradition, modernity has in some key areas been the period where Christian tradition itself has been exposed as resting on a misreading of scripture.

Stott's discussion of this area is notable for its humility – he frankly admits that modern evangelicals will have central cultural blind spots that will become apparent only to posterity, and which in all likelihood he is himself unable to recognize:

> The first step towards the recovery of our Christian integrity will be the humble recognition that our culture blinds, deafens and dopes us. We neither see what we ought to see in scripture, nor hear God's Word as we should, nor feel the wrath of God's anger against evil. We need to allow God's Word to confront us, disturbing our security, undermining our complacency, penetrating our protective patterns of thought and behaviour, and overthrowing our resistance.[35]

It is fundamental to his approach that the faithful Christian should always be open to the possibility that their interpretation of scripture is wrong. If not only our ability to correctly evaluate our culture and discern where it may be under God's judgement, but also our ability to recognize what scripture is actually saying in the first place and to hear the way it speaks to us today is affected by cultural preconceptions, a humble willingness to revisit our interpretation when we become aware that other faithful Christians come to different conclusions seems essential: 'What will posterity see as the chief Christian blind spot at the end of the twentieth century? I cannot say with any degree of certainty, because of course I share in the same myopia myself.'[36] This is clearly the implicit approach behind Stott's discussion of same-sex relationships in *Issues* (1984), even if some of the later editions make this stance less clear. He acknowledges that the church has homophobically misread scripture in the past – up to and including mistranslating passages. He respectfully engages with Christians (including liberals) who interpret scripture differently, being open to challenge where appropriate, and without denouncing as heretical those who he continues to disagree with.

Stott's broad approach here, of a basic humility regarding our own ability to evade the influence of our culture, and a willingness to engage in genuine dialogue with the world, connects well to the less dystopian vision of modernity we have been exploring. If we really are all expressive individuals now, then it should be no surprise that the church is not some culture-neutral oasis where interpretation of scripture is somehow always able to be objectively reasonable as long as we try really hard. The difficulty with more dystopian conservative evangelical approaches like Trueman's is that they have a tendency to assume that the faithful conservative Christian has already seen through the deceptions of the anticulture. Although Trueman is very willing to critique the way in which progressive Christians have adopted the thought patterns of expressive individualism, there is little sign of Stott's humble awareness that in all likelihood he too has adopted them. It is this sort of assumption that conservatives have an objective perspective and can see through the cultural naivety of progressives that lies behind the attempts of those such as Webb to set out rules of interpretation by which transcultural truth can be clearly and easily separated out from its cultural components. The possibility that conservatives themselves might already have cultural blind spots that affect their evaluation of scripture is never seriously considered. The idea that traditionally held Christian beliefs and practices (like holy war, torture and slavery) might have been the result of cultural misreadings by previous generations who similarly thought they simply followed the clear meaning of scripture is downplayed. In fact, the entire thrust of Trueman's analysis militates against this sort of understanding. By identifying modernity exclusively with the progressive cultural forces that conservatives are opposing, it is axiomatic that a conservative interpretation of scripture on sexuality is understood as necessarily countercultural. Therefore conservatives feel confident that unlike their opponents they are not blinded by culture.

However, Stott's warning to beware complacency and have humility in our interpretation of scripture is double-edged, not simply a club to beat progressives with. Progressives themselves routinely argue that conservative interpretation of scripture is affected by cultural blinkers in that it is interpretation done within the traditions, practices and thought-patterns of a homophobic institution. Progressive evangelicals such as Jim Wallis and Shane Claiborne have long been arguing that conservative interpretation of scripture exhibits significant cultural blindspots in its willingness to accommodate capitalism.[37] Stott's point, considered properly, demands that *both* accusations be taken seriously. Progressive interpretation of scripture may be overly influenced by the politics and theories of the New Left. Conservative interpretation of scripture may be overly influenced by the historical traditions of a homophobic institution. Humility in interpretation as outlined by Stott means accepting that both of these are possible, and that those advancing each interpretation would be convinced that they were simply stating the obvious truth of scripture. The fact is that, as Taylor reminds us, modernity is multifaceted and does not speak with one voice. Attempting to rule out cultural blind spots by imagining we can somehow, while under the influence of our culture, discern exactly how to spot if we are being affected by it is ludicrous. It plays into the delusion that we are able somehow to step outside our culture and evaluate it objectively. As MacIntyre reminds us however, we should not think we need to approach this as individuals. Making sense of our traditions (and perhaps even more so, letting our traditions make sense of us) is something we do as a community in the broadest sense, not just in the comfort of our own echo chambers. To get a clearer perspective on where our cultural blind spots are, progressives and conservatives need each other's help.

Curated communities

To explore this a little further means returning to consider once again what modernity really is if we are viewing it through less dystopian lenses. If, following Taylor, we recognize it as multivocal and containing the potential for both creative and destructive impulses, this means that the dismantling of the authoritative voices and institutions of the past does not have to be understood as the final death of culture but could be the site of emergence of something new. I also want to consider MacIntyre's insight that identity and moral values in modernity are shaped through dialogue in community, in a genuinely conversational process where the individual discerns who they are in conversation with others. As Trueman has noted, this is bad news for those who want to insist on models of identity and moral value being established by an external authority. However, it does not mean reducing everything to personal preference (indeed MacIntyre's entire approach is designed to avoid this), rather the discipline of discerning identity and values in dialogue is designed to enable us to get beyond personal or institutional bias to step closer to what is actually true. As Taylor argues, although the undermining of external authorities might seem to rule out a place for God, in fact all the evidence is that God keeps breaking into modernity and confronting us in all sorts of unexpected places. If we were to consider what sort of community this feels like if it were a church, and how the authority of scripture functions within it, it would be a church that feels more like a group of people engaged in Bible study than a congregation listening to an expository sermon. There is not a single institutionally appointed source of authority, no single authoritative interpreter of scripture, but this does not mean that there are no limits to individual interpretation. The limits are found in dialogue with a community that recognizes that scripture has authority and holds each other to account for the truth that is discerned in scripture and the way that is lived out in all of their lives.

To give a little more detail to this broad outline, I want to draw on the work of the sociologist Anthony Giddens, particularly on his *Modernity and Self-identity* and *The Transformation of Intimacy*. In these books, Giddens explores the changes that have happened in our experience of relationships and our sense of identity in modernity. For our purposes Giddens' work is very useful because it aligns substantially with the outline of modernity I have already sketched out, while opening up new ways of understanding what is going on. It allows us to recognize the sorts of cultural changes registered by Trueman, Taylor and MacIntyre without seeing modernity through a dystopian lens. Like Taylor and Trueman, Giddens prefers to emphasize the continuities between earlier and later modernity rather than stress the late twentieth century as a decisive breaking point, preferring the terminology of 'high' modernity and, as we shall see, his analysis has some broad similarities to theirs. He accepts Trueman's basic point that modernity means the dethroning of authoritative institutions – your denomination and local church, your civic authorities and predominant national culture and so on. Crucially for our purposes, however, he does not see this as the emergence of an anticulture, and the possibility of meaningful society and culture disappearing. He sees this as a shift to a different sort of culture where identity, relationships and authority function differently. He is far more interested in what this cultural iconoclasm makes room for – if people no longer take their identities, moral codes and outlooks from these authoritative sources, where do they get them from? As we shall see, his answer bears striking similarities to MacIntyre – people get their identity, outlook and moral values from communities, though Giddens adds the caveat that in modernity these are self-selected and curated communities. Unlike Trueman, therefore, Giddens sees modernity as the site of emergence of something new. It is essentially constructive, about building a new form of culture. By exploring what this culture looks like, I will demonstrate that in the church it looks very like modern evangelicalism.

Giddens argues that one of the defining features of modernity, after the removal of the older and static institutions as authorities, is the increasing interconnection between globalizing cultural, social and structural movements and personal identities and dispositions. Given that he was writing in the early Nineties, his understanding is eerily prescient of the development of social media and the prevalence of smartphones. In the modern age he argues, global trends and social movements can shape our individual identities and outlooks directly (and in turn our own life choices can shape global trends) in a way that is unprecedented: 'Self-identity today is a reflexive achievement. The narrative of self-identity has to be shaped, altered and reflexively sustained in relation to rapidly changing circumstances of social life, on a local and global scale.'[38] So, a young person trying to understand who they are can now draw through various media on a bewildering array of models and examples from across the world and throughout history. Similarly, the novel life choices of families in apparently obscure communities can come to the attention of people all over the world, and may end up creating new patterns of relationship that have huge influence. And this is not peripheral to modernity, some sort of accidental by-product, this is a central expression of what modernity *is*. Modernity is all about freeing people from an inherited social order and empowering them to build something new that gives them more control over their lives and their future. Far from seeing the pluralism of modernity as a dystopia, then, Giddens sees it as a hotbed of creative opportunities.

Faced with this wide array of options, the self has become a reflexive bricolage project – we are actively engaged in a process of exploring and creating ourselves as we engage with wider society. We do this by curating the media we access, by making choices about what experts we choose to give credence to, by choosing goals and lifestyles, and even in moments of crisis by reinventing ourselves by reconstructing a new sense of self from early experiences that have more consonance with our changed circumstances. In all of this, we look increasingly for expertise and guidance more to systems and people who are abstracted from our context (counsellors, medical or educational professionals, Christian authors or bloggers, media personalities, scientists, artists) than we do to the systems and people who are part of our context (family, friends, local community). Our communities are chosen and curated by us (we may choose to attend a church across town rather than our local one, and supplement their teaching by regularly listening to a Christian podcast). The similarities to MacIntyre's approach here become clear – in modernity we find our identities and moral values in dialogue with a community (though MacIntyre would want to stress that our communities help us understand the choices we make rather than stressing our free choice as independent agents). Where Carson sees this sort of pluralistic pick-and-mix approach as inherently unstable and implicitly undermining any meaningful authority, Giddens sees it as genuinely good and enriching for society.

Giddens is keen to point out that, although this disembedding from the local significantly undermines traditional sources of authority, it is not a negative development. It genuinely opens up new possibilities for people that would otherwise be unavailable to them:

> The expansion of abstract systems [experts not limited to our local community] creates increasing quanta of power – the power of human beings to alter the material world and transform the conditions of their own actions. The reappropriation of such power provides generic opportunities not available in prior historical eras.[39]

In modernity people genuinely have more freedom, more agency, than ever before and this is a good thing. As Trueman concedes, recognizing human dignity is a Christian value. In a church context, we might note that although your local church leader may have less influence over you than was the case in pre-modernity this is not necessarily a bad thing. You are able to access a far wider range of teaching, worship and spiritual guidance that allow you to develop a deeper and richer understanding than would have been available to any churchgoer in a pre-modern setting. There are obvious dangers in adopting this sort of highly individualistic pick-your-own-expert approach to faith, as Trueman and MacIntyre have pointed out, but the fact is we are already all-in on this strategy. All of us who go to a church outside our parish, who read mass-produced books written by people we have never and will never meet, who listen to podcasts and worship songs from the other side of the world, attend national conferences, or who regularly network with other Christians across the country are living a fundamentally modern faith.

Modernity, sexuality and relationships

Giddens is particularly interested in the effect of modernity on sexuality and relationships, and I want to spend some time setting out his understanding in detail, as it demonstrates the unavoidable extent to which evangelicals are already thoroughly modern in their values, pattern of life and sensibilities even (perhaps especially) at the point where Trueman believes they are seeking to hold to a pattern of sexual morality that is countercultural. Giddens not only shows why Trueman is right to discern modern sexuality as representing a distinctively new way of inhabiting our identities, he also shows why gay and queer sexualities and the modern evangelical sexual morality both represent accommodation to this distinctively modern sexuality. It is important to engage with his analysis to highlight both the continuities with and the distinctions from

Trueman's analysis. The first thing to highlight is that there is significant common ground. Both Giddens and Trueman make the point that sex and sexuality are omnipresent in modernity and seen and experienced as of fundamental importance to identity. For both, then, the fact that debates around sexuality have become political hot potatoes in church and society is unsurprising. Giddens would further agree with evangelical dystopian analysis, like that of Carson, Guinness and Harrison that one of the defining characteristics of modernity is being a guilt-free and self-referential society and this significantly undermines traditional moral codes. Traditional moral values, like other forms of inherited identity and lifestyle, depend on a strong sense of extrinsic authority – the sense that there is something outside yourself that has a right to tell you what to do, and that if you set yourself against that authority you should rightly feel guilty for doing so. Giddens agrees that modernity has been profoundly corrosive of the authority claims of anything outside the self and that this is a central part of what modernity is, not an accidental by-product. It is a fundamental part of enabling people to have the freedom to choose their own identity and their own lifestyle that the authority of anyone else to make those choices for you must be undermined.

Giddens highlights the way in which our relationship with our bodies, our understanding of our own identity, and the way we interact publicly and privately with others are all understood to be negotiated aspects of our sexuality in modernity. In other words, sexuality is one of the primary ways in which the modern project is explored, celebrated and extended. Here, par excellence, we see the self engaged in a project of creative exploration, building an identity in the most personal and intimate areas of life that is in dialogue with global trends and influences and where we typically look for guidance, not from family or local community, but from experts (doctors, church ministers, counsellors, films, novels, pornography, books, media personalities) who are abstracted from our situation. The life patterns articulated by individuals are then shared with the world (through social media, through agony aunt columns, through TV shows, through research) and form global movements. In the realm of sex and relationships we see the modern connection between the personal and the global in its purest form. So far, Giddens appears to offer a very similar analysis to Trueman.

It is in examining the distinctive expressions of sexuality and relationship in modernity that a distinction between the two becomes clear. Giddens describes sexuality and relationships in modernity by reference to the terms 'plastic sexuality' and 'the pure relationship'. In both cases Giddens carefully traces the history and development of these notions back into earlier centuries, but argues that the legal, social and technical circumstances for their full realization have only been in place in the second half of the twentieth century. In broad terms this is a similar analysis to that of Trueman, who also uses the terminology of plasticity to describe identity in modernity. In regard to sexuality, Giddens writes:

> plastic sexuality is decentred sexuality, freed from the needs of reproduction. It has its origins in the tendency ... strictly to limit family size; but it becomes further developed later as a result of the spread of modern contraception and new reproductive technologies.[40]

It is important to recognize here that although 'plastic sexuality' is an analysis that can be applied to individual expressions of sexuality (thus we might regard someone who describes themselves as 'pansexual' to be exemplifying a plastic sexuality), Giddens is clear that 'plastic sexuality' describes *all* expressions of sexuality in modernity.

This is where a distinction between Giddens and Trueman becomes apparent, deriving from Trueman's ambiguity around the extent to which we really are all expressive individuals now. Trueman seems to regard understandings of plasticity in sexuality (which for him is exemplified by trans identities) as a deathwork that should (and therefore by implication can) be kept out of the church:

If, as Rieff claims, sexual codes are definitive of cultures, then an abandonment of Christian sexual morality by the church can be done only on the basis of a rejection of the sacred framework of Christianity and at the loss of Christianity as a meaningful phenomenon.[41]

For Giddens however, plasticity in sexuality is hardwired into modernity. We all have plastic sexualities now, even if we choose to express them in less dramatic ways. Plastic sexuality in Giddens' terms is not necessarily an ever-changing and obviously changeable sense of your own sexual identity, or a choice of a non-traditional sexual identity. Rather it is an expression of the effects of modernity in your sexual identity: the disembedding of the individual from inherited patterns, from connection in and obligation to their local community and kinship structures, and a simultaneous proliferation of options and choices of lifestyle from which the individual is encouraged and empowered to explore and create their own identity – all of this is expressed in a sexuality that is plastic. This does not necessarily mean that every individual is constantly reshaping their sexuality (though modernity creates the conditions within which that level of fluidity is possible), but that in modernity every individual's sexuality is always defined and negotiated by themselves in dialogue with others as one of a range of options and choices of lifestyle. This means that (to an extent never before true) our understanding and expression of our own sexuality has to be conscious and deliberate – even if not experienced as chosen, it is always a refusal of other options. 'Straight' sexuality only requires articulation or explanation when other options are recognized. The emergence of plastic sexuality as an omnipresent fact of our culture is the end of a culture where a straight cis-gendered understanding is regarded as the 'default'.

In Giddens' analysis therefore, everyone necessarily has a plastic sexuality in terms of their sexual identity. However, he would also suggest that we all have a plastic sexuality in our sexual practice, irrespective of whether that falls inside or outside

Trueman's 'Christian sexual morality'. To describe sexuality in modernity as plastic means it is a privatized sexuality detached from unchosen external obligation or review. This does not mean that an individual cannot choose to accept the authority of a traditional sexual ethic, simply that this is a choice to an extent that was unimaginable in pre-modern settings. There is no necessary cultural connection to reproduction, or to wider kinship structures or moral codes. Gay and queer sexualities in many senses seem the perfect example of this, being sexual relationships that in most cases do not allow for reproduction without the involvement of donor sperm, eggs, and perhaps a surrogate, and have on the whole proceeded without any need for public or private approval of their families or wider communities. However, it is a mistake to see gay sexualities as in some way distinct from straight sexualities in this regard. All sexuality in late modernity is plastic, and it is largely in the sexuality of straight women that plastic sexuality first emerged, as a liberation of female sexuality from male control. The introduction and wide accessibility of safe and reliable birth control, which separated sexuality from reproduction for straight women, and increased legal and financial freedoms allowing women independence from their families were some of the key drivers of the emergence of plastic sexuality. Evangelical acceptance that a married couple might delay having children or decide not to have them at all because they are prioritizing their careers, and that they should not have children unless they both want to is a manifestation of plastic sexuality. So also would be their decision to use contraception in order to have sex purely for pleasure with no possibility of conception. Both of these were regarded as breaches of Christian sexual morality in pre-modern cultures.

Corresponding to the notion of 'plastic sexuality' is the 'pure relationship', which Giddens introduces as the ideal form of romantic relationship in modernity:

> It refers to a situation where a social relation is entered into for its own sake, for what can be derived by each person from

a sustained association with another; and which is continued only in so far as it is thought by both parties to deliver enough satisfactions for each individual to stay within it.[42]

The pure relationship represents an ideal towards which modern relationships (especially marriage) aspire, expressing disconnection from external obligation and the empowering of the individual to choose their own identity and lifestyle. The pure relationship is one in which the relationship exists as much as possible simply for the mutual enrichment and enjoyment of the two individuals concerned, being the purest expression of love and the best location for the expression of sexuality. The pure relationship is easily recognized in the form of a 'dating culture' that is omnipresent in modernity. Prior to the increasing independence of women in the mid-twentieth century, as Giddens makes clear, courting was surrounded by societal expectations (and often governed by parental permission), and was expected to result in marriage. It is clear that some of the twentieth-century changes in divorce law, culminating in the no-fault divorce, also reflect this shift in cultural understanding. It is also reflected, however, in the decision in the 1980 ASB marriage service to allow a couple to choose whether to use a form of vows including the promise by the bride to 'obey'.

Once expressed in these terms, it is clear that modern evangelicals, as much as anyone else, would tend to understand sexuality and relationships as operating within a culture defined in this way, even if they acknowledge this by defining biblical understandings in opposition to the more extreme parameters of it.[43] Defining 'biblical marriage' as a deliberately chosen option that operates in tension with the expectations of wider society is distinctly different from the understanding held by pre-modern (and even early modern) cultures. Evangelical understandings of marriage have likewise often tended to uncritically mirror the modern ideal of the pure relationship, stressing the way in which a mutual relationship of sexual intimacy brings the greatest possible fulfilment to the couple. Stott's description of the mystery of one flesh union in marriage is a good example: 'much more than a union of bodies; it is a blending of complementary personalities through which, in the midst of prevailing alienation, the rich created oneness of human being is experienced again'.[44] This evangelical idealization of the pure relationship as the highest human fulfilment is obviously problematic for single people, prompting a robust challenge from Ed Shaw:

> Our response to the sexual revolution going on outside our doors has sadly just been to promote sexual intimacy in the context of Christian marriage. And to encourage people to keep it there by promising this will then deliver all the intimacy they've ever wanted.[45]

This discussion of sexual identity and morality in modernity highlights the difference between Giddens and Trueman. As I have noted, Trueman's refusal to really accept that 'we are all expressive individuals now' means that in this area he deliberately downplays the obvious extent to which evangelicals are already thoroughly modern. Ultimately this encourages a misunderstanding that evangelicals are somehow able to keep modernity at bay, remaining a pre-modern or trans-cultural enclave unaffected by the surrounding dystopia. Not only is this unhelpful in that it prevents evangelicals from truly recognizing the extent to which they are immersed in and blinded by their culture, it also encourages a demonization of that surrounding culture. This is particularly the case in regard to sexual identity and activity, where analyses like Trueman's play into a myth of a monstrous modernity that evangelicals are assumed to be holding back. If the insights of Taylor, MacIntyre and Giddens are given appropriate weight however, and we accept that evangelicals are just as much part of modernity as everyone else, this encourages a more hopeful evaluation of the possibilities of faith and Christian faithfulness within modernity.

Progressives and conservatives as modern Christians

In all the above I have deliberately discussed in some detail the extent to which evangelicals are undeniably modern in their thinking and practice at the point where Trueman insists most strongly that they are not really expressive individuals. It is at this point that we can return to an understanding of what a Christian community in modernity actually looks like. I suggested earlier that, following MacIntyre, it might be understood best as more like a Bible study than a Bible exposition. Christian community in modernity is multivocal, it is about working together as a community to do the characteristically modern work, in Giddens' terms, of curating our own identities, discerning what our values and practices should be. Against Trueman's understanding that the authority of scripture and tradition could have no part in this, because expressive individuals will not be bound by history or external authority, I argue with MacIntyre that expressive individuals discern and recognize the authority of scripture and tradition in conversation. Indeed, tradition itself is best understood as a conversation around the discernment of authority and what submitting to that authority might look like. Once understood in this way, I would argue that both progressives and conservatives are in fact already part of such self-chosen communities and that their engagement with the sexuality debate is a textbook example of what modern Christian communities in a conversation with tradition about authority looks like.

At this point it becomes clear that the rhetoric of 'progressive' and 'conservative' (and even more so 'traditionalist' and 'revisionist') is in many ways profoundly unhelpful. Both sets of labels give the impression that the dividing line can be drawn on acceptance of modernity. Progressives or revisionists are those who see at least some aspects of modernity as a good thing and wish to move the church into greater harmony with the modern world. Conservatives or traditionalists are those who see at least some aspects of modernity as a bad thing and wish to encourage the church to resist harmonization with the modern world. But if we really are 'all expressive individuals now' it is a mistake to understand self-styled progressives as somehow more modern and self-styled conservatives as somehow less modern. Both are equally modern, in a modernity that in Taylor's terms is hugely diverse and includes currents that are profoundly opposed to the modern project while counter-intuitively still themselves being thoroughly modern.

Progressives and conservatives are both simultaneously accommodating and resisting different aspects of modernity, with the differences between them more differences of degree than absolute distinctions. Even those working hard to swim against the tide and adopt self-consciously traditional practices and understandings are, by virtue of doing so, engaging in a very different and modern sort of activity than their pre-modern ancestors (who had no such array of easy alternatives) did. In modernity any identity or lifestyle is to a great extent a chosen or constructed one rather than an inherited one – even the choice to adopt an 'inherited' identity is a choice. In fact, as is apparent from a closer examination of conservative evangelical groups, there are key respects in which the 'conservative evangelical' identity is just as much a departure from an inherited evangelical identity as the 'progressive evangelical' one. It is notable, for example, that they are unlike the conservative evangelicals of the early twentieth century, the ones engaged in a civil war with liberal evangelicals. Twenty-first-century evangelicals are almost entirely charismaticized, have a markedly more relaxed attitude to alcohol and the cinema, seek to root their approach to scripture in critical scholarship, and make common cause with traditional Catholics (with some of them happily engaging with Catholic spirituality).

A clear example of the inherent limitations of the progressive/conservative dichotomy as a tool for analysis is shown in the recent Save the Parish movement. In July 2021 Canon John McGinley spoke at the MultiplyX church planting conference to encourage fresh missional thinking in the Church of England and a vision of 10,000 new churches. In his speech he mentioned certain 'key limiting factors' holding back mission: 'a building, and a stipend, and long, costly college-based training for every leader'.[46] McGinley is a senior conservative evangelical leader – part of the leadership of New Wine. His statement therefore represented a not untypical conservative evangelical perspective – that radical change to models of theological training, lay leadership and non-church-centric forms of mission are the way forward. His comments, however, provoked a significant movement to resist such changes, spearheaded by Marcus Walker, the Anglo-Catholic rector of St Bartholomew the Great and supported by Giles Fraser, who founded Inclusive Church. Counter-intuitively then, 'conservatives' are here advocating iconoclastic action: undermining the authority of the clergy and doing away with traditional residential theological colleges, where the 'progressives' are resisting any attempt to modernize archaic structures.

The fact is that 'conservative' and 'progressive' are both thoroughly modern identities, representing different acts of discernment by different communities of the spiritual dangers and opportunities of modernity and therefore different ways to inhabit it. 'Conservatives' have tended to rhetorically position themselves as defending a historic faith in the face of a changing world, adopting a stance of resistance in the area of sexual and gender identity and a cautiously guarded relationship with critical biblical scholarship but have happily accommodated modernity in areas like consumerism and managerial understandings of Christian leadership. 'Progressives' have preferred to understand themselves as embracing the world as it is and setting aside all that inhibits the advance of the kingdom, accommodating changed understandings of sexual and gender identity and a range of critical approaches to scripture, yet have also resisted modernity in a variety of areas ranging from popular culture to consumerism to modernization of church structures and worship. The fact that these are broad-brush caricatures, and any individual conservative or progressive probably has their own slightly different portfolio of resistance and accommodation to modernity simply underlines the point. Both accommodate and resist modernity at different points.

Ultimately progressives and conservatives have much more in common with each other than with the majority of the population who do not go to church. From the perspective of modernity as a whole, *all* Christians adopt a broadly similar stance that is distinctively different from those around them. They go to church and engage in organized worship. They express allegiance to a religious institution (with whatever caveats they feel necessary – and both liberals and evangelicals are well known for the caveats they place on this). They adopt a selection of spiritual practices (prayer, reading the Bible, worship, confession). These similarities are far more significant in distinguishing a peculiarly Christian stance within modernity than the theological disagreements between liberal and conservative Christians which seem to each sharply differentiate them. This is even more the case when it comes to contrasting progressive and conservative evangelicals. The challenge now is to recognize that rather than staying in curated communities of their own, they may be called to acknowledge that the church is bigger than that, and to dare to step into the common ground they share with each other. The conversation we are now called to have requires us to start to listen to those we do not agree with, in the expectation that if we sit together humbly we may find that the gospel speaks to both of us in Stott's words in a way that is both true and new.

Conclusion: The phony war over modernity

Since the Sixties, evangelicals have been painting themselves a picture of modernity as a monstrous enemy – an anticulture that is utterly inhospitable to faith and makes living a faithful life impossible. Alongside this, they have also been quietly accommodating various strands of modernity, most visibly in their worship and organizational structures, but also less visible areas, including a reframing of sexual morality around the centrality of fulfilling relationships rather than procreation. Growing conflict with more self-consciously progressive

Christians has encouraged an increasingly oppositional stance, which denies the possibility of common ground. Despite this, the reality is that conservatives and progressives are both equally natives of modernity, and modernity itself is multivocal, and by no means as inhospitable to faith as writers like Carson or Trueman suggest.

Notes

1 Trueman, Carl R., 2022, *The Rise and Triumph of the Modern Self*, Wheaton: Crossway, p. 390.
2 Trueman, 2022, p. 25. On this point Trueman is following Taylor strongly.
3 Niebuhr, H. Richard, 1951, *Christ and Culture*, London: Harper & Row.
4 Stott, John, 1984, *Issues Facing Christians Today*, 1st edn, Basingstoke: Marshall, Mogan & Scott, p. 24.
5 Guinness, Os, 1973, *The Dust of Death*, Westmont, IL: InterVarsity Press, p. 317.
6 Davison Hunter, James, 1992 *Culture Wars: The Struggle To Define America*, New York, Basic Books, pp. 112–13.
7 Schaeffer, Francis, 1990, *Trilogy*, Westmont, IL: InterVarsity Press, p. 132.
8 Schaeffer, 1990, p. 269.
9 Carson, Don, 1996, *The Gagging of God*, Westmont, IL: InterVarsity Press, p. 48.
10 See Brown, Callum G., 2009, *The Death of Christian Britain*, 2nd edn, London: Routledge.
11 See Paul, Ian, 2022, 'Dear Richard Coles, whither the Church of England?', *Psephizo*, 22, April, https://www.psephizo.com/life-ministry/dear-richard-whither-the-church-of-england/ (accessed 14.2.2023).
12 Trueman, 2022, pp. 88–9.
13 Trueman, 2022, pp. 401–2.
14 Trueman, 2022, pp. 402–6.
15 Trueman, 2022, p. 45.
16 Trueman, 2022, p. 387.
17 Harrison, Glynn, 2016, *A Better Story: God, Sex & Human Flourishing*, Westmont, IL: InterVarsity Press, p. 10.
18 Harrison, 2016, p. 179.
19 Taylor, Charles, 2007, *A Secular Age*, London: Harvard University Press, p. 727.

20 Taylor, 2007, p. 743.
21 Taylor, 2007, p. 745.
22 MacIntyre, Alasdair, 1981, *After Virtue*, London: Duckworth, p. 221.
23 MacIntyre, 1981, p. 222.
24 MacIntyre, Alasdair, 1988, *Whose Justice? Which Rationality?*, Duckworth: London, p. 391.
25 Trueman, 2022, p. 399.
26 Bebbington, David, 1999, *Evangelicalism in Modern Britain*, London: Routledge.
27 Holland, Tom, 2019, *Dominion: The Making of the Western Mind*, London: Little Brown, p. 517.
28 Trueman, 2022, p. 90.
29 Cornwall, Susannah, 2017, *Un/Familiar Theology: Reconceiving Sex, Reproduction and Generativity*, London: Bloomsbury, p. 19.
30 Stott, John, 1992, *The Contemporary Christian*, Westmont, IL: InterVarsity Press, p. 27.
31 Stott, 1992, p. 28.
32 Stott, 1992, p. 28.
33 Stott, 1992, p. 29.
34 Stott, 1992, pp. 191–2.
35 Stott, 1992, p. 193.
36 Stott, 1992, p. 192.
37 Wallis, Jim, 2005, *God's Politics*, New York: Harper Collins; Claibourne, Shane, 2006, *The Irresistable Revolution*, Grand Rapids: Zondervan.
38 Giddens, Anthony, 1991, *Modernity and Self-identity*, Cambridge: Polity Press, p. 215.
39 Giddens, 1991, p. 139.
40 Giddens, 1992, *The Transformation of Intimacy*, Cambridge: Polity Press, p. 2.
41 Trueman, 2022, p. 406.
42 Giddens, 1992, p. 58.
43 Roach, Jason, 2019, *Swipe Up*, Epsom: The Good Book Company.
44 Stott, 1984, p. 311.
45 Shaw, 2015, p. 75.
46 Leader comment, 9 July 2021, 'Key limiting factors', *Church Times*, https://www.churchtimes.co.uk/articles/2021/9-july/comment/leader-comment/leader-comment-key-limiting-factors (accessed 14.2.2023).

5

Advice to a divided church

In the preceding chapters I have argued that the sexuality debate has become weaponized in a culture war over responses to modernity between conservatives and progressives. This has become particularly problematic for evangelicals because it threatens to split evangelicalism itself, redrawing the map of tribal identities to create a broad conservative grouping (uniting conservative evangelicals with traditional Catholics) and a broad progressive grouping (uniting progressive evangelicals with broad liberals and liberal Catholics). This is already occurring at a political level, where progressive evangelicals join Inclusive church to campaign alongside those of very different spiritualities, while conservative evangelicals seek to arrange alternative episcopal structures in parallel to traditional Catholics. Conservative evangelical tendencies to paint a dystopian vision of modernity have encouraged the idea that this division between conservatives and progressives is a first order issue of faithfulness in which the fate of the Western church (and on some readings Western civilization as a whole) is at stake. However, this crude division into a choice between two options conceals the significant common ground between all those on both sides (and particularly between conservative and progressive evangelicals), as well as the significant divisions and gradations of position within each side.

My argument, drawing on the insights of Girard, is that the pressures of a scandalized conflict have pushed progressives and conservatives to see each other as monstrous rivals, each determined to eradicate the other. This has created a simplistic binary opposition that makes it very hard to recognize the possibility of common ground, encouraging the perception that the two sides are utterly unlike each other. In the words of Rowan Williams: 'everyone believes they are a persecuted minority. And this is not a situation that encourages easy and honest communication. It is a situation that cries out for scapegoats.'[1] And scapegoats are not hard to point to in a politicized situation where some are more vulnerable than others. Girard suggests that scapegoats are most naturally found in marginal groups, those who are both 'like us' (and so can plausibly be blamed for the difficulties we all face) and yet 'not like us' (and so can be blamed without implicating ourselves). Gay people in evangelical settings are in this sense natural scapegoats, as are any evangelicals in conservative settings who publicly question the consensus position. In progressive settings evangelicals might easily themselves be scapegoats. It is very easy for these people to become isolated, subjected to disproportionate levels of scrutiny, forced to prove their bona fides, and excluded from supportive networks and positions of respect and authority. Some find themselves without support from their church community at precisely the moment that they are going through significant personal struggles. Even if they manage to prove that they are still among the faithful, the shadow of past accusations may continue to hang over them.

If this is the situation in which we as a church now find ourselves, I would suggest that the pressing ethical question before us is not actually the question of sexuality itself, but the question of how we live together as brothers and sisters in Christ in the midst of all this. The question of what church looks like in modernity and how we cope with seemingly irreconcilable disagreement within it becomes the most pressing one. In this final chapter, I want to reflect on the implications of the analysis I have set out for where we find ourselves as a church. If the sexuality debate really represents a proxy war over responses to modernity, with progressives and conservatives operating within the distorting influence of scandalized communities, what might be a faithful Christian response to this? How do we defuse the sexuality debate?

Avoid overly swift declarations that adherence to particular positions represent first order issues of faith

I have been clear from the start that I feel that one of the keys to defusing the sexuality debate is for conservatives to stop suggesting that refusal to adhere to the consensus position represents a first order issue of faith. By now the reasons for this should be clear. In the first place, I do not believe it is a position that can be maintained with integrity on any of the grounds commonly appealed to. The consensus position is a modern position in church policy based on a modern interpretation of scripture. It cannot be found anywhere prior to the mid-twentieth century, as its basic form – an acceptance of homosexual orientation (and condemnation of homophobia) combined with a condemnation of homosexual acts (and restatement of the ideal of heterosexual marriage) only makes sense in the context of the decriminalization of homosexuality. The pattern of biblical interpretation on which it is based is derived from twentieth-century scholarship, focusing on different passages read differently than in earlier tradition. In addition, maintaining the understanding that refusing to accept the consensus position is faithlessness to the gospel has catastrophic effects. It has a chilling effect on genuine discussion of sexuality in conservative contexts. It makes it very difficult for evangelicals to express honest doubt and ask open questions without risk that they will be ostracized by their own churches. This has the undoubted effect that many wrestling with difficult questions (including those coming to terms with their own sexuality) will not reach out for support to their church community at the times when they are most in need of that support. The lack of a space within existing structures where people can easily express doubt, or say that they don't know what they think about these divisive issues without being marginalized encourages people to either stay silent or leave. This creates on the one hand silent groups of people within conservative churches whose lived experience of faith is increasingly at odds with a party line with which they feel forced to assent, and on the other it creates conservative orphans, who no longer feel entirely at home in conservative contexts where their doubts cannot be expressed, and yet who are too conservative to feel entirely at home in more progressive contexts. If we want to ensure that all members of our churches flourish, and are serious about facilitating a genuine conversation around these questions, neither is a healthy outcome.

As I stated above, I think that the position of O'Donovan and others that in as much as the sexuality debate is a debate concerning the doctrine of marriage (as opposed to a particular pastoral policy towards sexual relationships) it can be considered a first order issue of faith bears more serious consideration. This requires an important caveat, however, in that asserting a first order issue is being discussed here is to make a claim about the status of the issues being discussed and the care that should be taken in finding a resolution, it is not in itself a claim in favour of any particular pastoral policy. (It is therefore perfectly possible to recognize that the doctrine of marriage is of first order significance and to argue for a change in pastoral provision for those unable to enter into marriage without this constituting a call for doctrinal change.) This was the case made in the paper on 'The Church of England's Doctrine of Marriage' that was released prior to the February Synod, which did not explicitly rule out a place for prayers of blessing, but noted concern that the draft prayers should not depart from doctrine.[2] The paper's presentation of the doctrine of marriage was notable, however, for its failure to recognize the extent to which the current practice of the Church of England represents a modernization of older tradition. (Ironically underlined by the fact that it acknowledged that Common Worship reordered and reworded the traditional goods of marriage without seeing this change as in any way doctrinally significant.) Instead, the (negative) influence of modernity was traced in secular understandings of marriage, with its influence on church practice unacknowledged. Neither the conservative nor the progressive understandings of marriage and sexuality can claim to stand in unbroken continuity with what went before, even if the conservative position can claim the distinction of representing the status quo of church policy. Both represent to some degree modern developments of earlier tradition. A claim that first order issues are at stake, therefore, should represent an invitation to discussion of these matters, not an attempt to draw a line under them. I think in making this distinction, evangelical intuitions that something of the gospel is at stake can be recognized, without closing off the possibility of genuine conversation. In fact, recognizing the significance of the issues should encourage a willingness to persevere with conversation rather than rushing to seek to close it down.

Depolarize the debate

In my engagement with the work of Girard I noted the way his analysis suggested the existence of a tight cycle of reciprocity between monstrous rivals expressed as a rush to extremes. Essentially, Girard's point is that the mirroring between rivals in scandalized communities acts as an accelerant towards violence. Every provocation sparks a retaliation that will tend to be disproportionate, because every perceived act is associated with all those that went before it, and the response is to the sum of all of them, rather than just to that particular act. In addition, the perceived monstrousness of the rival works to legitimate the worst possible interpretation being placed on their actioms. Thus, an ill-considered act (CEEC releasing a video at a time that might seem to prejudice the outcome of the LLF process), is given the worst possible interpretation (this is a deliberate attempt to torpedo the entire initiative because evangelicals are determined to avoid gay people being heard). This can then prompt a disproportionate response in suggestions that it constitutes homophobia and hate speech, as was noted by Andrew Goddard in his analysis of responses to the video.[3]

It is important to recognize the way this dynamic operates in scandalized community, because it means that unless conscious steps are taken to avoid it, this will always become the default response. It takes conscious interventions by people on both 'sides' to depolarize debate and avoid such incidents (that will inevitably occur) from becoming moments of escalation. Recognizing that these moments of escalation are the flashpoints when fallout occurs, often in the form of people disconnected from the original incident being scapegoated, should motivate both 'sides' to prevent this. Instead, steps can be taken to slow down the cycle, creating space and time where listening can occur. Goddard's article provides examples of this sort of intervention. In the first place the article itself represents Goddard, as a conservative, noting the temptation he feels to respond with a hermeneutics of suspicion, but instead seeking to listen to and understand the responses to the video rather than immediately leaping to a response that is defensive or tends towards escalation. Second, Goddard draws attention to interventions by progressives to de-escalate some of the responses of their own 'side', drawing attention to Colin Coward's post in a Facebook group to encourage people not to respond with horror and panic. Resisting the pressure towards immediate and often suspicious or defensive responses to perceived acts of provocation by the other 'side' gives space for more moderate voices on both sides to be heard.

Avoid demonizing modernity

I have spent some time critiquing the conservative dystopian tradition of writing about modernity, in particular by engaging in depth with Trueman. Although I have set out some more pragmatic reasons for this (in terms of the way in which it disables the possibility of genuine debate, identifying progressives with fundamentally anti-Christian values), I have also sought to show that this represents a genuine misunderstanding of modernity. A proper understanding of modernity has to take into account Taylor's insights that it is inescapable and also multivocal. Identifying the church as somehow not native to modernity is a fundamental mistake, leading to denial of the ways in which the church is thoroughly modern, as well as a refusal to recognize the extent to which modernity embodies Christian values. It encourages evangelicals to understand themselves as resisting modernity, setting them in an oppositional relationship to the world around them, and deepening their inability to recognize the critiques made of them by liberals.

I have explored in some depth the extent to which conservatives demonize modernity, but it should be recognized that there is also a progressive version of this tendency. The progressive dystopian vision is one that is expressed well in films like *Don't Look Up* (2021). From this perspective, modernity is recognized as the triumph of destructive capitalism, the eclipse of human beings in all their diversity and individuality by soulless corporate power. It is axiomatic that this eclipse of the human is oppressive, marked by the triumph of patriarchy, homophobia and racism. It is also destructive of the planet and embeds structural inequalities. All of this is facilitated by spineless institutions (including churches and governments) who justify it to the masses and by a myriad of distractions and entertainments to prevent anyone from recognizing their oppression or calling anyone to account for it. Once this dystopian vision is accepted, the institutional church is regarded as a patsy of oppressive powers and corporate interests, too often offering justifications for doing nothing and offering worship as entertainment rather than inspiration for action. The progressive resisting modernity understands themselves as a resistance cell in occupied territory, often becoming overly concerned with checking the bona fides of cell members to ensure they haven't been compromised. The dynamics are therefore much the same – the extent to which non-progressive modern institutions and individuals embody genuinely Christian values is not recognized, and the degree to which the faithful themselves are inevitably modern is often implicitly denied (despite high levels of anxiety over the degree to which use of corporate products and social media platforms represents compromise).

Both of these versions of the dystopian vision of modernity represent an oversimplification and denial of the existence of substantial common ground between conservatives and progressives. Both make genuine conversation with 'the other side' impossible. There can be no compromise with a modernity that is an anticulture and fundamentally opposed to the gospel. Both tend towards a denial of hope and the possibility of redemption and encourage extreme solutions. Both massively reinforce tendencies towards self-righteousness and discourage genuine self-awareness.

Stay humble and listen openly

I highlighted the approach of Stott as one that is grounded in humility about our own theological convictions and a commitment to genuine listening to others. Although Stott himself had a key role in establishing the consensus position, his outlook always remained conciliatory. His frank admission of the extent to which we are all blinded by our culture, even when it comes to discerning what we consider to be the plain truth of scripture, is a powerful insight. Conservatives have frequently been willing to admit that they have made mistakes in their actions and even in the way they have done their theology – the current reappraisal of the place of single people in very family oriented evangelical churches is a good example here. However, there has not often been a willingness to admit that conservative culture can produce misreadings of scripture that conservatives are themselves unable to recognize. Conservatives are alert to the possibility of progressive misreadings of scripture due to cultural blindness, as in Gagnon's rejection of homosexual readings of David and Jonathan's relationship as 'specious connections' made by people removed from the cultural context of scripture.[4] However, as we have seen, Gagnon's confidence in his own ability to discern the cultural blind spots of others seems not to produce a corresponding awareness that he might himself have such blind spots. Thus, in his discussion of Jesus' reference to the creation narratives in Mark 10.1–12, he critiques any attempt to read a modern progressive viewpoint into Jesus' silence on homosexuality on the basis that as an observant Jew Jesus can be assumed to hold to the law in Leviticus. However, he then proceeds himself to read into Jesus' silence an acceptance of his own modern conservative theology of gender complementarity in Genesis.[5] This presumption that although our opponents are blinded by their cultural preconceptions we can discern what is clearly there in scripture is far from Stott's reminder that those who went before us were likewise very sure that scripture legitimized torture, or crusades or slavery. They saw things in scripture that today we simply don't, spinning a whole theology to justify the enslavement of Africans out of speculation about the descendants of Ham.

None of this requires that we let go of our theology, or indeed that we are not required to do all we can to discern the true meaning of scripture. It certainly didn't stop Stott himself from advancing a very similar understanding to Gagnon of the significance of the creation narratives. However, it does require us to hold our theology a little more humbly, in the awareness that we might be wrong, and our brothers and sisters in Christ who disagree with us might have seen something we are blind to. It means listening openly to the perspectives of others in the expectation that in so doing we might both discover something new.

A degree of humility is appropriate given the inarguable historical fact that no one in the history of the church has argued for this particular position of church policy on the basis of this particular set of interpretations of scripture prior to the mid-twentieth century. The failure to acknowledge the extent to which this is true has tended to discourage conservatives from acknowledging the necessity of repentance for an earlier homophobic tradition, and it has encouraged a denial of the need for careful scholarship, discernment and dialogue in establishing the consensus position. If it is not recognized that condemnation of homophobia is a distinctive moral stance taken by modern evangelicals, it starts to feel like a defensive denial of being homophobic rather than a positive statement of conviction. This does not help gay people, whether they are progressive or conservative, to feel that their safety and acceptance is recognized as a priority. Similarly, an airy assurance that scripture is clear and no further debate is necessary does not accurately represent the reality of the process by which conservative evangelicals have themselves arrived at their understanding, and discourages genuine dialogue with progressives. This is both because the complexity of questions of interpretation (which as we have seen in places turn on the likely derivation and cultural referents of words in millennia old dead languages) are effectively denied, and because evangelicals are themselves disempowered from engaging in such dialogue.

Recognize the complexity of the conversation

I have at several points highlighted the extent to which the sexuality debate is about far more than sexuality, and in many ways is a proxy for a conversation about the way the church should respond to modernity as a whole. The Living in Love and Faith resources have helpfully highlighted the extent to which questions of identity (including gender identity), sexuality, relationships and marriage (and therefore also family) are all interrelated. It is also clear that questions of where authority is situated within the church (that is, who is it who is doing the discernment here – is it the church as a whole, General Synod, the House of Bishops?), how we should appropriately interpret and draw on scriptures and tradition that contain pre-modern cultural emphases we now reject, and what weight we should give to the insights of the wider secular world are central to all of these areas. This means that rather than a simple ethical question with a yes/no answer, the church is in reality engaged in an extended conversation about a variety of interrelated areas of doctrine and practice, as well as an even more divisive debate about the appropriate tools and methodology to employ in having this debate (and who should ultimately have the last word in it). It is entirely possible to find that, for example, those who agree on sexuality do so on profoundly different grounds, so that their apparent agreement masks a far deeper disagreement about the authority of scripture or the relevance of the voices of the marginalized. Similarly, we should not be surprised to find that some of those who apparently disagree on sexuality may do so within an almost identical framework of doctrinal commitments and understanding of the authority of scripture and tradition, so that their apparent disagreement masks a deeper commonality. The inherent complexity of the debate needs to be acknowledged, rather than ignored in the rush to find a resolution. Otherwise, and inevitably, the underlying questions will resurface, still unaddressed, in whatever the next issue might be, making it equally intractable. The dream of a quick resolution allowing everyone to move on, although comforting, is utterly impossible.

Viewed from this perspective, it is clear that the 'slippery slope' arguments often articulated by conservatives actually contain an important insight, despite progressive dismissals as scaremongering. There *is* a genuine sense in which reimagining the theology of marriage in order to accommodate same-sex couples inevitably also opens the door to consideration of whether polyamorous relationships should be recognized, as scholars like Cornwall have acknowledged. Although there is no necessary sense in which the one follows from the other, the questions are genuinely interconnected in all the ways I have outlined above. Acknowledging the genuineness of this interconnection of issues, however, also makes clear that conservative insistence on maintaining the status quo is effectively a use of power to avoid engaging with a hugely destabilizing debate. Conservative evangelical analysis of modernity as an anticulture suggests that there is significant anxiety that making *any* concessions to modernity in the area of sexuality would lead to the disintegration of the church and undermine the truth of the gospel. As Trueman argues: 'an abandonment of Christian sexual morality by the church can be done only on the basis of a rejection of the sacred framework of Christianity and at the cost of the loss of Christianity as a meaningful phenomenon'.[6]

Conservative evangelical insistence that adherence to the consensus position is a first order issue and cannot be reopened is thus to some degree also an insistence on not having an open conversation about understandings of gender, or the family, or the extent to which our treasured Christian traditions have become compromised by misreading of scripture.

Yet the wider conversation about church and discipleship in modernity is already happening, and the refusal to engage in it is in itself to assert a (sometimes unexamined) position in the conversation. Understandings of sexuality in conservative circles have become determined by the consensus position, which includes within it a set of interpretations of passages of scripture that cannot now easily be challenged. This is hugely problematic when, as we have seen, sexuality relates closely to a huge range of the other questions facing the church in modernity. Gender identity is fast overtaking sexuality as one of the most significant touchstone issues of the day, and not only have evangelicals only just begun to address it, they are approaching discussions with a response that is partly predetermined because debates on sexuality so closely relate to gender. As we have seen, the consensus position has encouraged an approach to sexuality that revolves around a particular understanding of gender complementarity, adherence to which is now regarded as a first order issue of faithfulness. In the sexuality debate, the goodness of gender difference as God's created intention is affirmed (allowing only heterosexual marriage) whereas difference in sexuality is regarded as a result of the Fall. All sexualities, both gay and straight, can plausibly be described as fallen, allowing gay people to be fully accepted as people while being excluded from marriage. Binary gender is seen as an inherent part of our creation in the image of God – communicating eternal truths. As Ed Shaw remarks in regard to sexuality, 'a binary distinction was made right back in the beginning by the God who made us all. Gender is not a social construct, it's a divine one.'[7] However, when this interpretation is applied to the trans debate, it produces a far more hardline position. The consensus position does not deny that gay people experience what they experience, and should be loved and accepted as they are. By contrast, this understanding of gender lends itself to an interpretation where trans, genderfluid or intersex people are believed to not really experience what they experience and therefore cannot be loved and accepted as they say they are. Traces of this line of argument are clear in documents like the EA's *Transsexuality*, which asserts:

> We affirm God's love and concern for all humanity, but believe that God creates human beings as either male or female. Authentic change from a person's given sex is not possible and an ongoing transsexual lifestyle is incompatible with God's will as revealed in Scripture and in creation.[8]

It is clear then, that treating the sexuality debate as a distinct and closed question that can be treated as an already-settled first order issue of faith is likely to turn a whole range of other unforeseen but interrelated issues into first order issues where the answer is already known before a serious discussion has already begun. As Girard reminds us, scandals are opportunistic, with existing scandals readily encompassing the new ones. An obvious consequence of this is that the trans debate is entered by conservative and progressive evangelicals who have already been through escalating hostilities. A trans young person in an evangelical church that has never really addressed issues of gender identity will therefore find themselves walking unsuspectingly into the heavily militarized warzone of a conflict that began decades before they were born about questions very different from their own.

What sort of church are we called to be?

Ephraim Radner, exploring some of the difficult history of the discipline of ecclesiology, discusses an underdeveloped understanding found in Luther's theology that the sins of the church make up part of the suffering of Christ on the cross, and that the church in following Christ, will also share in these sufferings.[9] It is in embracing the sufferings of Christ (which include its own self-inflicted wounds) that the church truly follows in the footsteps of its saviour. In developing this theme, Radner notes that it potentially undermines some of Luther's other theological impulses, given that he was at the time trying to identify where the 'true church' could be found. However, Radner sees this as a key biblical theme, that in the midst of division the church is called to submission to the needs of the other, citing 1 Corinthians 12.24–26, written to a deeply divided church:

> But God has so arranged the body, giving the greater honour to the inferior member, that there may be no dissension within the body, but the members may have the same care for one another. If one member suffers, all suffer together with it; if one member is honoured, all rejoice together with it.

He seeks to challenge the myth that faithfulness to Christ is expressed in separation from our brothers and sisters in the church with the notion that faithfulness to Christ may actually be best expressed in self-sacrificially continuing to bear with one another. Romanticizing division as an expression of faithfulness may be an ever-present protestant temptation, but it is one we can ill afford at present.

Where scripture might seem hard to interpret in regard to sexuality, it is very clear on how we should relate to fellow believers and even to our enemies and those we feel are persecuting us. Paul, commenting on the lawsuits between believers among the Corinthians, asks the question: 'why not rather be wronged?' The radical challenge of the gospel is that we should more readily allow ourselves to be wronged and disadvantaged than allow division within the community to become politicized. It is very easy to convince ourselves that we are defending a point of principle so significant that how we treat others is a lesser concern. The uncomfortable truth is that this side of eternity the normal life of the church necessarily looks more like sacrificial compromise, messy political deals and failure to be all we are called to be, than any of us like to admit. Fleeing from this to an idealized pure church where we are free to be ourselves without compromise with those who are our brothers and sisters and yet are utterly different from us may simply be another manifestation of expressive idealism.

As Hays notes:

> For the foreseeable future we must find ways to live within the church in a situation of serious moral disagreement while still respecting one another as brothers and sisters in Christ. If the church is going to start practicing the discipline of exclusion from the community, there are other issues far more important than homosexuality where we should begin to draw a line in the dirt: violence and materialism for example ... the questions are so difficult that we should receive one another as brothers and sisters in Christ and work toward adjudicating our differences through reflecting together on the witness of Scripture.[10]

Notes

1 Williams, Rowan, 2003, 'Archbishop's Presidential Address to General Synod, York, June 2003', http://rowanwilliams.archbishopofcanterbury.org/articles.php/1826/archbishops-presidential-address-general-synod-york-july-2003.html (accessed 14.2.2023).

2 'The Church of England's Doctrine of Marriage', signed by a variety of bishops, the majority of whom are evangelical http://www.sswsh.com/uploads/The-Church-of-Englands-Doctrine-of-Marriage-paper.pdf (accessed 05/04/23).

3 Andrew Goddard noted this response of the Christians for LGBTI+ equality Facebook group, https://www.fulcrum-anglican.org.uk/articles/the-beautiful-story-reflections-and-response/?fbclid=IwAR1-oyRSP7WX3C3v2Lo-IyOtn7gulyq9KPA2u-9ngunVVUo1oBZvtVTpu74 (accessed 14.2.2023).

4 Gagnon, Robert A. J., 2001, *The Bible and Homosexual Practice*, Oxford: Abingdon, p. 154.

5 Gagnon, 2001, p. 194.

6 Trueman, Carl R., 2022, *The Rise and Triumph of the Modern Self*, Wheaton: Crossway, p. 406.

7 Shaw, Ed, 2015, *The Plausibility Problem*, Nottingham: Inter-Varsity Press, p. 84.

8 EA, 2000, *Transsexuality*, Carlisle: Paternoster, pp. 84–5.

9 Radner, Ephraim, 2017, *Church*, Eugene, OR: Wipf & Stock, pp. 155–6.

10 Hays, Richard, 1996, *The Moral Vision of the New Testament*, Edinburgh: T&T Clark, pp. 400–1.

Appendix

A timeline for evangelicalism and sexuality in the twentieth and twenty-first centuries

Before the Sixties

- Sexual minorities actively discriminated against, with male homosexual acts illegal.
- Wide recognition that this legal framework was open to abuse and not fit for purpose.
- Internal battles within evangelicalism lead to splits between conservatives and liberals, with the conservatives becoming inward-looking, disengaging from the Church of England and wider society, focused purely on evangelism and discipleship, and creating parallel structures as alternatives to existing bodies.

1861 *Offences Against the Person Act* makes any same-sex activity by men punishable by imprisonment.

1919 Formation of IVCF (later UCCF) as conservative evangelical student movement separate from the more liberal SCM.

1922 Formation of BCMS (later Crosslinks) as conservative evangelical missionary society separate from the more liberal CMS.

1957 Wolfenden Report published recommending decriminalization, supported by CofE.

APPENDIX

The Sixties and Seventies

- Legal reform of sexual rights is just a part of wider explosion of cultural change and the emergence of the 'permissive society'. Sections of the church embrace this change, other sections resist it.
- Church attendance begins to go into steep decline.
- Under the influence of John Stott, conservative evangelicals re-engage with church and society.

1964   Fountain Trust founded. Charismatic revival sweeps historic denominations in Britain, causing rifts within evangelicalism.

1967   *Sexual Offences Act* decriminalizes same-sex activity between two men over 21 in private.

1967   National Evangelical Anglican Conference in Keele expresses an outward-looking evangelicalism re-engaging with the Church of England and issues of social justice.

1969   Stonewall Riot in the US signals the emergence of a new self-assertive and countercultural gay identity.

1971   Nationwide Festival of Light founded to stand against the permissive society.

1974   First Greenbelt festival.

1975   London Institute for Contemporary Christianity founded.

1976   Gay Christian Movement founded (becomes LGCM in 1986).

1977   *Third Way* magazine established.

1977   *Gospel and Spirit* published, marking a rapprochement between charismatics and conservative evangelicals.

1977   True Freedom Trust established to support gay christians wanting to escape a 'homosexual lifestyle'.

1979   GCM establishes an evangelical fellowship.

The Eighties and Nineties

- A significant reactionary cultural shift in Thatcher's Britain accompanied by the AIDS epidemic signals a sharp but temporary step backwards in public acceptance of sexual minorities.
- The first British Social Attitudes Survey in 1983 shows 50% believe same-sex relationships are always wrong. By 1987 this had increased to 64%. By 1994 there was a return to 1983 levels of acceptance.

1980   GCM publishes liturgy for a same-sex blessing service.
1981   Gloucester Report on Homosexual Relationships published. Condemned by both conservatives and liberals.
1982   *The Churchman* publishes articles on biblical scholarship by James Dunn perceived as too liberal, prompting the dismissal of the editor who goes on to found *Anvil* as a more liberal evangelical journal.
1983   Evangelical Assembly established in order to guide the evangelical 'party' (not least in General Synod, established in 1970).
1984   Action for Biblical Witness in Our Nation founded, concerned to uphold family values.
1987   ABWON successfully has LGCM ejected from their offices under accusations of promoting promiscuity, pornography, child abuse and drug use.
1987   General Synod motion declares homosexual genital activity is sinful.
1988   *Local Government Act* passed. Section 28 bans the promotion of homosexuality as a pretended family relationship.
1989   Osbourne Report on Sexuality suppressed by church and never published because seen as too liberal.
1990   George Carey calls for a Decade of Evangelism to reverse decline in church attendance.
1991   *Issues in Human Sexuality* published.

APPENDIX

1992   The Ordination of Women as priests prompts the establishment of Reform as a Conservative Evangelical campaigning organization.

1993   Gerald Bray condemns 'open evangelicals' as unfaithful to Christ and uncommitted to evangelism in an editorial in *The Churchman*.

1994   The Children's Society announces it will no longer accept Gay and Lesbian couples for fostering.

1994   Homosexual age of consent lowered to 18 after pressure from the EU.

1996   ABWON and Reform oppose the LGCM service of thanksgiving in Southwark Cathedral, threatening to withhold quota payments if it went ahead.

1998   Lambeth Conference passes Resolution 1:10 declaring homosexual practice is incompatible with scripture but homophobia should be condemned following careful coordination between Western and Southern conservatives.

Into a new millennium

- With the election of New Labour in 1997 there was a cultural shift in mood towards greater acceptance of diversity.
- By 2000 BSA polling showed only 37% of the population thought same-sex relationships were always wrong, and 34% thought they weren't wrong at all.
- By 2010 a majority of the population felt that same-sex relationships were never or rarely wrong and only 20% felt they were always wrong.
- As a swift succession of legal changes came into effect protecting the rights of queer people, conservative evangelicals mobilized to try to prevent change and then to mount legal challenges when they felt the rights of Christians to hold contrary views were infringed. Church leaders lobbied to prevent changes to marriage legislation.

2000 Ban on LGBT service in Armed Forces lifted.
2002 *Adoption Act* allows gay couples to adopt.
2002 Evangelical Archbishop George Carey replaced by liberal catholic Rowan Williams, known to be pro-gay. The appointment is lobbied against by conservative evangelicals and condemned unanimously by the CEEC, over the protests of Christina Rees, prompting her resignation. The CEEC All Soul's Day Statement declares sexuality is a first order issue and that leaders not holding to a conservative position should be opposed.
2003 Section 28 repealed.
2003 Abortive attempt to appoint the openly gay and partnered Jeffrey John as Bishop of Oxford stopped after evangelical campaigns against him. Anglican Mainstream and Fulcrum form in the fractious aftermath as respectively more conservative and more liberal evangelical groupings.
2003 Inclusive Church forms, initially as a protest against evangelical responses to Jeffrey John. Includes evangelical members.
2003 Openly gay and partnered Gene Robinson appointed as bishop in US episcopal church. Same-sex blessings happen in the episcopal church in Canada.
2004 *Civil Partnership Act* and *Gender Recognition Act* passed.
2007 Foundation of the Christian Legal Centre as pro bono legal support for Christians discriminated against on the basis of faith. Closely linked to the campaigning group Christian Concern, founded in 2008 (though previously part of the evangelical Lawyers' Christian Fellowship).
2008 Lambeth Conference so divided over sexuality that a rival Global Anglican Futures conference is held in Jerusalem, attended by bishops boycotting Lambeth. In their Jerusalem Declaration they announce the formation of parallel 'orthodox' Anglican structures, without formally declaring themselves in schism.

APPENDIX

2008 Open division between evangelicals at NEAC5 following a botched attempt by the CEEC chair to get the conference to adopt the Jerusalem Declaration.

2009 Anglican Mission in England launched by GAFCON as a parallel ecclesial structure for orthodox Anglicans. The group plants a number of churches and ordains its own bishop in 2017.

2010 *Equality Act* consolidates piecemeal protections already in law to make sexuality a protected characteristic under discrimination law.

2013 *Same Sex Marriage Act* passed. Following lobbying from the Church of England the legislation includes a 'triple lock' to make it impossible to be interpreted as permitting same-sex marriage in church. In the process this for the first time makes this illegal.

2013 Prominent Baptist evangelical Steve Chalke declares his support for same-sex marriage. Evangelical Alliance disaffiliates both from him and his Oasis organization.

2013 Pilling Report starts a two-year Listening Process within the CofE through a series of shared conversations between delegates from all dioceses. The Process is regarded with deep scepticism by both liberals and conservatives, with Reform advising its members to boycott it.

2014 Diverse Church formed by gay evangelical Sally Hitchener to support young queer people in the church.

2017 House of Bishops summary report following the Listening Process restates the modest changes recommended by Pilling. Rejected by Synod following lobbying against it by both sides. Prompts the announcement of a new teaching resource on sexuality: Living in Love and Faith.

2020 Living in Love and Faith published as a book and web-based teaching resource.

2022 Stephen Croft, evangelical Bishop of Oxford, becomes first evangelical bishop to publicly call for acceptance of same-sex marriage in lead up to debate on LLF at General Synod.

2023   February General Synod approves the use of prayers of blessing for same-sex couples, provided these do not depart from CofE doctrine. This necessitates new pastoral guidance, making *Issues in Human Sexuality* obsolete.

Further reading

I recognize that people wanting to read further likely fall into two groups: people wanting to look up one of the specific references I make, and people simply wanting to explore some of the themes I've opened up a bit further. So for Chapters 1–4 I've listed two sorts of further reading: suggested reading (for people wanting to read other books about these themes) and bibliography (full details of the key books I've referred to in each chapter). Books appear in the list for the chapter where they are first mentioned.

Chapter 1 – Evangelicals talking about sexuality

Suggested reading

Loader, William, 2013, *Making Sense of Sex*, Cambridge: Eerdmans.
Mazo Karras, Ruth, 2017, *Sexuality in Medieval Europe – Doing Unto Others*, 3rd edn, London: Routledge.
Skinner, Marilyn B., 2014, *Sexuality in Greek and Roman Culture*, 2nd edn, Chichester: Wiley Blackwell.

Bibliography

Atkinson, David, 1979, *Homosexuals in the Christian Fellowship*, Oxford: Latimer House.
Bailey, Derrick Sherwin, 1955, *Homosexuality and the Western Christian Tradition*, London: Longmans.
Board of Social Responsibility, 1979, *Homosexual Relationships – A contribution to discussion*, London: CIO.
Davidson, Alex, 1970, *The Returns of Love*, Westmont, IL: InterVarsity Press.
Field, David, 1976, *The Homosexual Way – A Christian Option?*, Bramcote: Grove Books.

Foucault, Michel, 1981, *The History of Sexuality, Volume 1: The Will to Knowledge*, trans. Robert Hurley, London: Penguin.
Gagnon, Robert A. J., 2001, *The Bible and Homosexual Practice*, Oxford: Abingdon.
Gill, Sean, ed., 1998, *The Lesbian & Gay Christian Movement*, London: Cassell.
Harrison, Glynn, 2016, *A Better Story: God, Sex & Human Flourishing*, London: InterVarsity Press.
Hays, Richard, 1996, *The Moral Vision of the New Testament*, Edinburgh: T&T Clark.
House of Bishops, 2013, *Report of the House of Bishops Working Group on Human Sexuality GS1929*, 'The Pilling Report', London: Church House Publishing.
Moberley, Elizabeth R., 1983, *Homosexuality: A New Christian Ethic*, Cambridge: James Clark & Co.
Moss, Roger, 1977, *Christians and Homosexuality*, Exeter: Paternoster.
Rogers, Eugene F., ed., 2002, *Theology and Sexuality*, Oxford: Blackwell.
Scanzoni, Letha Dawson and Mollenkott, Virginia Ramey, 1978 *Is the Homosexual My Neighbour?*, New York: Harper Collins.
Stott, John, 1984, *Issues Facing Christians Today*, 1st edn, Basingstoke: Marshall, Mogan & Scott.
White, John, 1977, *Eros Defiled*, Westmont, IL: InterVarsity Press.
Williams, Craig A., 2010, *Roman Homosexuality*, 2nd edn, Oxford: Oxford University Press.

Chapter 2 – Evangelicals talking about scripture

Suggested reading

Brown, Peter, 1988, *The Body and Society*, New York: Columbia University Press.
O'Donovan, Oliver, 2009, *A Conversation Waiting to Begin*, London: SCM Press

Bibliography

Augustine, 1992, *Confessions*, trans. Henry Chadwick, Oxford: Oxford University Press.
Barth, Karl, 1958, *Church Dogmatics, Vol. 3/1*, trans. G. W. Bromiley and T. F. Torrence, Edinburgh: T&T Clark.

FURTHER READING

Bonnington, Mark and Fyall, Bob, 1996, *Homosexuality and the Bible*, Cambridge: Grove Books.

Bradshaw, Timothy, ed., 1997, *The Way Forward?*, Cambridge: Eerdmans.

Brownson, James V., 2013, *Bible, Gender, Sexuality*, Grand Rapids: Eerdmans.

Calvin, John, 1573, *Commentary on Corinthians*, trans. John Pringle, https://ccel.org/ccel/calvin/calcom39/calcom39.xiii.ii.html (accessed 14.2.2023).

CEEC, 2022, *How Important are Our Differences?*, https://ceec.info/resources/gods-beautiful-story/ (accessed 14.2.2023).

Chrysostum, John, 2016, 'Homily 4 on Romans', in *Nicene and Post Nicene Fathers*, Series 1, Vol. 11, ed. Philip Schaff, Edinburgh: Eerdmans.

Countryman, L. William, 1988, *Dirt, Greed and Sex*, Philadelphia: Fortress.

Cranfield, C. E. B., 1975, *Commentary on Romans*, Vol. 1, Edinburgh: T&T Clark.

Davidson, Richard M., 2007, *Flame of Yahweh*, Peabody: Hendrickson.

Douglas, Mary, 1966, *Purity and Danger*, London: Routledge.

Foucault, Michel, 2021, *The History of Sexuality Volume 4: Confessions of the Flesh*, trans. Robert Hurley, London: Vintage.

Goddard, Andrew and Horrocks, Don, 2012, *Biblical and Pastoral Responses to Homosexuality*, London: Evangelical Alliance.

House of Bishops, 1991, *Issues in Human Sexuality*, London: Church House Publishing.

House of Bishops, 2003, *Some Issues in Human Sexuality – A Guide to the Debate*, London: Church House Publishing.

Louth, Andrew, ed., 2001, *Ancient Christian Commentary on Scripture: Genesis 1–11*, Westmont, IL: InterVarsity Press.

Lovelace, Richard F., 1978, *Homosexuality and the Church*, London: Lamp Press.

Paul, Ian, 2014, *Same Sex Unions*, Cambridge: Grove Books.

Pierce, Ronald W. and Westfall, Cynthia, eds, 2021, *Discovering Biblical Equality*, 3rd edn, Westmont, IL: InterVarsity Press.

Piper, John and Grudem, Wayne, 2021, *Recovering Biblical Manhood and Womanhood*, Wheaton: Crossway.

Roberts, Vaughan, 2002, *Together in Love and Faith? Should the Church bless same-sex partnerships? – A response to the Bishop of Oxford* https://2713aced-d665-4866-bcd0-8f7d81f2f5fe.usrfiles.com/ugd/2713ac_4f9a3958db324778b807e9507fb7c1b3.pdf (accessed 14.2.2023).

Schmidt, Thomas E., 1995, *Straight and Narrow?*, Westmont, IL: InterVarsity Press.
Stott, John, 1990, *Issues Facing Christians Today*, 2nd edn, London: Marshall Pickering.
Stott, John, 1999, *New Issues Facing Christians Today*, 3rd edn, London: Marshall Pickering.
Stott, John and McCloughry, Roy, 2006, *Issues Facing Christians Today*, 2006, 4th edn, Grand Rapids, Zondervan.
Thatcher, Adrian, ed., 2015, *The Oxford Handbook of Theology, Sexuality and Gender*, Oxford: Oxford University Press.
Third Lateran Council, edict 11, https://www.papalencyclicals.net/councils/ecum11.htm (accessed 14.2.2023).
Von Rad, Gerhard, 1961, *Genesis*, trans. John H. Marks, London: SCM Press.
Webb, William J., 2001, *Slaves, Women & Homosexuals*, Westmont, IL: InterVarsity Press.
Wright, David, 'Homosexuals or Prostitutes? The meaning of arsenokoitai', *Vigiliae Christianae* 38 (1984): pp125–53.

Chapter 3 – Evangelicals in conflict

Suggested reading

Bates, Stephen, 2004, *A Church at War*, London: I.B. Tauris.
Fleming, Chris, 2004, *Rene Girard*, Cambridge: Polity Press.
If you want to read some Girard directly, *I See Satan Fall Like Lightning* is the most accessible, but much of my thinking here has drawn more from *Battling to the End*.

Bibliography

Bray, Gerald, 1993, 'Editorial', *The Churchman*, 107 No. 4.
CEEC, 2020, *The Beautiful Story*, https://ceec.info/resources/the-beautiful-story/ (accessed 14.2.2023).
Evangelical Alliance, 1998, *Faith, Hope and Homosexuality*, London: Acute.
Girard, Rene, 2001, *I See Satan Fall Like Lightning*, trans. James G. Williams, Leominster: Gracewing.
Girard, Rene, 2010, *Battling to the End*, trans. Mary Baker, Michigan: Michigan State University Press.
Grenz, Stanley, 1998, *Welcoming But Not Affirming*, Louisville: Westminster John Knox.

Gumbel, Nicky, 1995, *Searching Issues*, Eastbourne: Kingsway.
Hill, Symon, 2011, 'Christianity & Homophobia in Britain Today', text of address to Camden LGBT Forum's *The Globalisation of Homosexuality* event May 2011, http://www.ekklesia.co.uk/node/14787 (accessed 14.2.2023).
Lee, Justin, 2013, *Unconditional*, London: Hodder.
Linzey, Andrew and Kirker, Richard, eds, 2005, *Gays and the Future of Anglicanism*, Winchester: O Books.
NatCen, 2013, *British Social Attitude Survey 30 Personal Relationships*, https://www.bsa.natcen.ac.uk/latest-report/british-social-attitudes-30/personal-relationships/homosexuality.aspx (accessed 14.2.2023).
Nolland, Lisa et al, 2008, *God, Gays and the Church*, London: Latimer Trust.
Reform, 2004, Letters, *Sunday Times*, November 28.
Runcorn, David, 2020, *Love Means Love*, London: SPCK.
Shaw, Ed, 2015, *The Plausibility Problem*, Nottingham: InterVarsity Press.
Vasey, Michael, 1995, *Strangers and Friends*, London: Hodder & Stoughton.
Vines, Matthew, 2014, *God and the Gay Christian*, New York: Convergent.
White, John, 1993, *Eros Redeemed*, Westmont, IL: InterVarsity Press.

Chapter 4 – Evangelicals talking about modernity

Suggested reading

Giddens, Anthony, 1992, *The Transformation of Intimacy*, Cambridge: Polity Press.
Holland, Tom, 2019, *Dominion: The Making of the Western Mind*, London: Little, Brown.

Bibliography

Bebbington, David W., 1999, *Evangelicalism in Modern Britain*, London: Routledge.
Brierley, Peter, 2006, *Pulling Out of the Nosedive*, London: Christian Research.
Brown, Callum G., 2009, *The Death of Christian Britain*, 2nd edn, London: Routledge.
Carson, D. A., 1996, *The Gagging of God*, Westmont, IL: InterVarsity Press.

Claibourne, Shane, 2006, *The Irresistable Revolution*, Grand Rapids: Zondervan.
Cornwall, Susannah, 2017, *Un/Familiar Theology: Reconceiving Sex, Reproduction and Generativity*, London: Bloomsbury.
Giddens, Anthony, 1991, *Modernity and Self-Identity*, Cambridge: Polity.
Guinness, Os, 1973, *The Dust of Death*, London: InterVarsity Press.
Hunter, James Davison, 1983, *American Evangelicalism*, New Brunswick: Rutgers University Press.
Hunter, James Davison, 1991, *Culture Wars*, New York: Basic Books.
Leader, 2021, 'Key limiting factors', *Church Times*, 9 July, https://www.churchtimes.co.uk/articles/2021/9-july/comment/leader-comment/leader-comment-key-limiting-factors (accessed 14.2.2023).
MacIntyre, Alasdair, 1981, *After Virtue*, London: Duckworth.
Niebuhr, H. Richard, 1951, *Christ and Culture*, London: Harper & Row.
Paul, Ian, 2022, 'Dear Richard Coles, whither the Church of England?', *Psephizo*, 22 April, https://www.psephizo.com/life-ministry/dear-richard-whither-the-church-of-england/ (accessed 14.2.2023).
Roach, Jason, 2019, *Swipe Up*, Epsom: The Good Book Company.
Schaeffer, Francis, 1990, *Trilogy*, Westmont, IL: InterVarsity Press.
Smith, Christian, 1998, *American Evangelicalism: Embattled and Thriving*, Chicago: University of Chicago Press.
Stott, John, 1992, *The Contemporary Christian*, Westmont, IL: InterVarsity Press.
Taylor, Charles, 2007, *A Secular Age*, London: Harvard University Press.
Trueman, Carl R., 2022, *The Rise and Triumph of the Modern Self*, Wheaton: Crossway.
Wallis, Jim, 2005, *God's Politics*, New York: Harper Collins.
Warner, Rob, 2007, *Reinventing English Evangelicalism*, Milton Keynes: Paternoster.
Webb, William J., 2001, *Slaves, Women & Homosexuals*, Westmont, IL: InterVarsity Press.

Chapter 5 – Advice to a divided church

Bibliography

Evangelical Alliance, 2000, *Transsexuality*, Carlisle: Paternoster.
Evangelical Alliance, 2011, *21st Century Evangelicals*, https://www.eauk.org/church/resources/snapshot/upload/21st-Century-Evangelicals.pdf (accessed 14.2.2023).

FURTHER READING

Goddard, Andrew, 2020, 'The Beautiful Story: Reflections and responses', *Fulcrum*, November 2020, https://www.fulcrum-anglican.org.uk/articles/the-beautiful-story-reflections-and-response/?fbclid=IwAR1-0yRSP7WX3C3v2L0-IyOtn7gulyq9KPA2u-9ngunVVU010BZvtVTpu74 (accessed 14.2.2023).

Radner, Ephraim, 2017, *Church*, Eugene: Wipf & Stock.

Williams, Rowan, 2003, 'Archbishop's Presidential Address to General Synod, York, June 2003, http://rowanwilliams.archbishopofcanterbury.org/articles.php/1826/archbishops-presidential-address-general-synod-york-july-2003.html (accessed 14.2.2023).

Index of Names and Subjects

abstinence/celibacy 67–8
  'consensus position' ix
  evangelical position 24
  faithful gay Christians 111
  higher calling than marriage 65
  homophobia and 13–14
Action for Biblical Witness to Our Nation (ABWON) 89, 92
adultery: sin but not crime 21
Alpha courses 85, 86, 106
American Psychiatric Association 95
Anglican Church *see* Church of England
Aquinas, Thomas of 59
  1 Romans and 42, 64
  homosexuality as sin 11, 20, 53–4
arsenokoitai, meaning of 51, 52
Atkins, Anne 92
Atkinson, David
  biblical arguments 35
  God's intention in creation 55
  Homosexuals in the Christian Fellowship 29–31
  interprets 'against nature' 55, 56
  Levitical laws 49
  Lot's daughters 42
  rejecting homophobia 17
  Stott and 32
Augustine of Hippo 67
  God's perfect intention 29–30
  On the literal interpretation of Genesis 66
  sexuality resulting from Fall 71
  Sodom in *Confessions* 41
authority, modernity and 145–9, 150

Bailey, Derrick Sherwin
  argument of 18–22
  consensus position and 26–8
  culture and scripture 104–5
  early responses to 22–5
  on Genesis 19 41, 42, 44

Homosexuality and
  the Western Christian
  Tradition 5–6, 14, 18–22
  interpretation of Romans
    54–5
  orientation *versus* practice
    51
  on *qadhesh/qudheshah*
    45–7
  rejecting homophobia
    15–17
  ritual sex in Leviticus 47–50
  scripture 29
  Stott and 32
  as 'tradition' 34
  unaddressed situations 21
Barth, Karl 61–2
The Beautiful Story video
A Better Story and 108–9
  biblical interpretation
    79–80
  moderation tendencies 106
  no space for single people
    110
  politics of 81–2
  release of 78–9
  today's issues and 80–1
Bebbington, David
  evangelicals and
    Enlightenment 134
  'The Great Reversal' 16
bestiality, Buggery Act and
  11
*A Better Story: God, Sex,
  and Human Flourishing*
  (Harrison) 1–2, 68, 107–8
  anticulture and 127–8

*The Bible and Homosexual
  Practice: Texts and
  Hermeneutics* (Gagnon)
  43, 102
Bible Churchman's
  Missionary Society (BCMS,
  later Crosslinks) 84
Bible, Gender, Sexuality
  (Brownson) 104
*Biblical and Pastoral
  Responses to
  Homosexuality* (Goddard
  and Horrocks) 45
biblical scripture
  applying to modern world
    141–5
  conservative clarity 38–40
  critical scholarship 40
  differences in interpretations
    57–8
  direct discussion of
    homosexuality in 39–40
  double listening 140
  Genesis narrative of
    marriage 3
  Genesis Sodom narrative
    41–5
  issues of interpretation 73–4
  Jesus on sexuality 58–60
  Levitical laws 47–50
  Mollenkott and Scanzoni
    28–9
  Pauline vice lists 50–7
  progressive evangelists
    104–5, 108
  Board of Social Responsibility
    24

INDEX OF NAMES AND SUBJECTS

Bonnington, Mark
  Genesis 19 43
  on Paul 56
Bray, Gerald, evangelical
  identity and 90
Britain
  Criminal Amendment Act
    (1885) 14–15
  decline in church attendance
    in 122
  Section 28 legislation 89
  Sexual Offences Act (1967)
    22
  see also Church of England
British Social Attitudes
  surveys on same-sex
    relationships 89, 91
Brownson, James 48
  Bible, Gender, Sexuality
    104
Buggery Act (1533) 5, 9
  a capital crime 11
  Reformation legislation 13

Calvin, John
  homophobia and 14
  homosexuality as sin 51
Campaign for Homosexual
  Equality 22
Carey, George, Archbishop of
  Canterbury
  bible-centred church 89
  replaced by Williams 91
Carson, Don 123
  The Gagging of God
    121–2
  guilt-free modernity 150

pick-and-mix identity 148
celibacy *see* abstinence/
  celibacy
Chalke, Steve 85, 101
charismatics 96
Christ and Culture (Niebuhr)
  116
Christianity
  anti-culture argument
    130–1
  Church's blind spots 141–2
  as modern 156–9
  Reformation and modernity
    134–6
Christians and
  Homosexuality (Moss)
  27–8
Chrysostom, John
  homophobic *Homily IV* 64
  interpretation of Romans
    66
Church Mission Society
  (CMS) 84
Church of England
  Bailey's argument and
    18–19
  Buggery Act and 13
  Civil Partnerships 91
  communication or
    apocalypse 109–11
  decriminalization campaign
    27
  early interpretation of
    scripture 39–40
  fracture lines 112–13
  gay clergy 22
  Gloucester Report 24

'Highton motion' 3
Homosexual Relationships
　35–6, 42, 55
policies on homosexuality
　4–5, 20, 91
Resolution 1.10 92
settlement on sexuality viii
theological training 157–8
UK Same-Sex marriage law
　3
Windsor Report 99
see also consensus position;
　conservative evangelicals;
　progressives
Church of England
　Evangelical Council
　(CEEC)
*How important are our
　difference?* video 58–60
policy politics 81–2
releases *The Beautiful Story*
　video 78–9
St Andrew's Day statement
　89, 91–2
video 62–3
Church Pastoral Aid Society
　96
Civil Partnership Act (2004)
　91
Claiborne, Shane 144
community
　churches 145–6
　modernity and identity
　　145–9
Confessions (Augustine of
　Hippo)
　reference to Sodom 41

consensus position
　biblical references ix
　communicating to
　　conservatives 107–8
　definition of ix, 2–6
　development of 25–8
　doctrinal truth 70–2
　importance of differences
　　69–70
　invention of tradition 34–6
　need for 28–31
　progressive rejection of 105
　questioned 98
　Sodom narrative and 42
conservative evangelicals
　alignment of 78
　Anglican identity crisis 83–6
　communication or
　　apocalypse 109–11
　complementary male-female
　　62–3
　compromise as betrayal 129
　confidence in scripture
　　38–40
　curated community 147
　definitions xi, 158
　Enlightenment and 134
　evangelical consensus
　　position 2–6
　extreme positions and
　　98–103
　first-order sexuality issue 4,
　　82–3, 96
　historical tradition 1
　issues of interpretation
　　57–8, 73–4
　Keele conference 84–5

INDEX OF NAMES AND SUBJECTS

Levitical laws 49–50
modernity and 116–17, 118–26, 155, 156–9
need for consensus 28–31
ordination of women 90
policy politics 81–2
redrawing the lines 105–8
rejecting homophobia 15–18
response to Bailey 24–5
sees dystopia 118–26
stance against homosexuality 90–6
worldliness as danger 118
The Contemporary Christian: An Urgent Plea for Double Listening (Stott) 138–45
contraception as sinful 11, 12
conversion therapy 98, 100
Corinthians, First Letter to
discussion of homosexuality 39
vice list 50–2
Cornwall, Susannah. *Un/Familiar Theology* 136–7
Countryman, L. William, *Dirt, Greed and Sex* 48
Cranfield, C. E. B., God's intention in creation 55
Cranmer Hall, blacklisted 97
Creation
God's intentions about sexuality 30
heterosexual marriage and 58–63

reunion of man and woman 32
see also Genesis, Book of
Croft, Steven, Bishop of Oxford
conservative to progressive journey 38
Together in Love and Faith 104
culture
anticulture 124–5, 133
blind spots 143–4
identity and community 146–9
Reformation and destruction 136
Stott's 'Transposing the Word' 141–5
'woke' 134–5
Culture Wars (Hunter) 119–20

Davidson, Alex (pseudonym), *The Returns of Love* 24, 111
Davidson, Richard M.
divine order in creation 57
Gagnon and 43, 44
Genesis interpretation 61
Levitical laws 49, 50
shrine prostitutes 46–7
Deuteronomy, Book of
discussion of homosexuality 39
qadhesh meaning 45–7
Dirt, Greed and Sex (Countryman) 48

Dominion: The Making of the Western Mind (Holland) 134–5
double listening 140–2
Douglas, Mary, *Purity and Danger* 48
The Dust of Death (Guinness) 119, 120

Ekklesia think tank 99
Elers, Revd Peter 23
equality
 but different 79
 male-female 60, 71
 see also homosexuality; women
Eros Defiled (White) 27–8, 93
Eros Redeemed (White) 93
Evangelical Alliance (EA)
 Biblical and pastoral responses to homosexuality 45
 Chalke and 101
 Faith, Hope and Sexuality 95
 Vasey and 97
evangelical civil war
 collapse of middle ground 100–3
 contested identity 86
 fracture lines 112–13
 modernity as hostile 122–3
 openness or apocalypse 109–11
 redrawing the lines 103–8
 rush to extremes 98–103

scandalized community 86–92
evangelicals *see* conservative evangelicals

Faith, Hope and Sexuality (Evangelical Alliance) 95
family and children
 Cornwall's approach 137
 'plastic' sexuality and 153–5
 as purpose of sex 9–10, 33, 66–9
 shifting emphasis 71
Field, David 24
 accepting homosexuals 17
 Atkinson and 29
 biblical arguments 35
 God's intention in creation 55
 The Homosexual Way 25–8
 Lot's daughters 42
 Stott and 32
Finch, Sarah, *God, Gays, and the Church* (with Nolland and Sugden, eds) 107
Fletcher, Joseph, *Situational Ethics* 22
Fountain Trust 84
Fraser, Giles 158
Freud, Sigmund 124
Fyall, Bob
 Genesis 19 43
 on Paul 56

The Gagging of God (Carson) 121–2

INDEX OF NAMES AND SUBJECTS

Gagnon, Robert A. J.
  The Bible and homosexual practice 43, 102
  Biblical concepts of sexuality 6
  Brownson's rebuttal 104
  divine order in creation 57
  Genesis 19 and 58
  Levitical laws 49, 50
  male-female difference 69
  on meaning of *qadhesh* 46–7
  one-flesh male-female union 60–1
  on Paul in classical context 56
  Paul's vice-lists 51
  re-evaluates ancient texts 18
Gay Christian Movement 22–3
Gay Liberation Front 22
Genesis, Book of
  discussion of homosexuality 39
  early church 'one flesh' teaching 63–9
  God's intention 29, 32
  heterosexual marriage 58–63
  human flourishing 108
  Jesus quotes 59–61
  one-flesh male-female union 60–1
  'sin against nature' 54
  Sodom narrative 19, 26–7, 41–5

Giddens, Anthony
  Modernity and Self-Identity 146–9
  'plastic' sexuality 149–55
  The Transformation of Intimacy 146–9
Girard, Rene
  possibilities 109
  scandalized communities 86–8, 98, 112
Global Anglican Future Conference 97
Gloucester report
  Homosexual Relationships 24
God
  creation intentions 29–30, 32, 55
  men not listening to 141–2
  rationalizing without 120
  God and the Gay Christian (Vines) 104
  God, Gays, and the Church (Nolland, Sugden and Finch, eds) 107
Greenbelt 85, 86
Gregory of Nyssa 65
Grenz, Stanley J., *Welcoming But Not Affirming* 102
Group for Rescinding the Act of Synod (GRAS) 90
Guinness, Oso 123
  Carson and 121
  The Dust of Death 119, 120
  guilt-free modernity 150
Gumbel, Nicky 85
  Searching Issues 106

Harrison, Glyn
  A Better Story 1–2, 68,
    107–8, 127–8
  guilt-free modernity 150
Hays, Richard
  Biblical concepts of sex 6
  Gagnon critiques 44
  Genesis 19 and 43, 58
  moral law distinctions 48
Henry VIII, Buggery Act and
    11
Higton, Revd Tony 89
Hill, Symon 99
HIV/AIDS 89, 103
Holland, Tom, *Dominion:
  The Making of the Western
  Mind* 134–5
homophobia
  AIDS epidemic 89, 103
  Chrysostom and 64–5
  Church's blind spots 142–3
  consensus position 26
  conversion therapy 98,
    100
  criminal law and 14–15
  execution and 14
  exorcism 98
  gay people within Church
    110–11
  LGCM report on 98–9
  pre-modernity 13–15, 133
  rejection of 1–2, 5, 15–18,
    21, 23, 26, 35
  sexuality debate and 83
  today's issues 80–1
  Williams plea for
    moderation 105–6

*Homosexual Relationships: A
  Contribution to Discussion*
  (C of E Gloucester report)
  24, 42, 55
*The Homosexual Way – A
  Christian option?* (Field)
  25–8
homosexuality
  abstinence and ix
  as an identity 33
  ancient views 31, 56
  conservative scriptural
    confidence 38–9
  as criminal 5, 11, 20–1
  desire 'against nature' 53–7
  as a disability 20–1, 21, 24,
    95
  doctrinal truth and 70–2
  evangelical stance against
    89–96
  exclusion from church life
    28
  gay rights activism 98
  God's intention and 30
  historical perspectives 39
  increasing social acceptance
    91
  malakoi and *arsenokoitai*
    51, 52
  meaning of *qadhesh* 45–7
  modernity of concept 12–13
  negative scriptural references
    3
  not addressed in *A Better
    Story* 108
  orientation *versus* act 8–9,
    13–14, 51, 55

INDEX OF NAMES AND SUBJECTS

penetration and 11, 19
'plastic' sexuality 149–55
pre-modern concepts 6–13
procreation and 33
provoked evangelicals and 92–6
revision of positions 4–5
ritual sex acts 47–50
shifting views of 15–21
as sin 41, 102
supposed promiscuity 94–5, 107
today's issues 80–1
trauma thesis 33
women and 13, 19, 54, 56
see also homophobia; marriage, same-sex
Homosexuality and the Western Christian Tradition (Bailey) 5–6, 14, 18–22
Homosexuals in the Christian Fellowship (Atkinson) 29–31
Honest to God (Robinson) 22
humility, Stott and 141–5
Hunter, James Davison
Carson and 121
Culture Wars 119–20
evangelicalism and modernity 122–3

identity
in modernity 145–9
'plastic' sexuality and 149–55

individualism, expressive 126–7, 134, 156
Intervarsity Fellowship 84
Is the Homosexual my neighbor? (Mollenkott and Scanzoni) 28–9
Israel, ancient
distancing ritual sex 47–50
shrine prostitutes 45–7
Issues Facing Christians Today (Stott) 6, 17, 31–5, 89
Church's blind spots 141–2
discussion of Genesis 19 43
fourth edition (with McCloughrey) 102
holiness and worldliness 116–18
on neglecting social justice 83–4
Issues in Human Sexuality (Stott) 3
bible-centred church 89
Genesis 19 43
Sodom narrative 42
Issues of Sexuality (Church of England) 78

Jesus Christ
culture and 116–17
Genesis and sexuality 3
Paul encounters 110
references to sexuality 58–61
Job, comforters of 139–40
John, Jeffrey, Bishop of Oxford 91, 107

Jude, *Testament of Naphtali* and 42

Karras, Ruth Mazo 9
Keele conference (1967) 34
Kings, First Book of
  discussion of homosexuality 39
  qadhesh meaning 45–7
Kinsey, Alfred
  acceptance of validity 26
  continuum of sexuality 29
  same sex attraction 8
Kirker, Richard, Windsor Report 99

Labourchere, Henry 14
Lee, Justin, *Unconditional: Rescuing the Gospel* 103–4
Lesbian and Gay Christian Mission (LGCM) 89
  evangelical civil war and 98
  evangelical fellowship 23
  report on homophobia 98–9
  thanksgiving service opposed 92
Leviticus, Book of
  qadhesh 46–7
  ritual sex acts 47–50
Linzey, Andrew, Windsor Report 99
Living in Love and Faith, *The Beautiful Story* video and 78–81
Local Government Act, Section 28 89

Lot: offers daughters 42
Love Means Love (Runcorn) 104
Lovelace, Richard F.
  God's intention in creation 55
  meaning of *malakoi* 52
Luther, Martin 68

McCloughrey, Roy, *Issues Facing Christians Today* (with Stott) 102
McGinley, Canon John 157–8
MacIntyre, Alasdair
  Christian modernity 156
  emotivism in moral discourse 131–2
  evaluating culture 145
  Giddens and 146
  moral values and community 145, 148
  Trueman and 123, 130
Macrina, celibacy of 65
malakoi, meaning of 51
March for Jesus 85, 86
marriage, heterosexual
  compared to celibacy 68
  consent and 72
  divorce and 59
  early church teaching 63–9
  Genesis and creation 58–63
  only appropriate context 2–3
  'plastic' sexuality and 153–5
  polygamy and monogamy 72

INDEX OF NAMES AND SUBJECTS

scriptural interpretation and 3
marriage, same-sex
  Civil Partnership Act 91
  consensus position ix, 26
  disbelief in 107
  doctrinal truth and 71–2
  early debates about 23
  non-recognition of 2–3
  unaddressed by Bailey 22
Marxism 124
masturbation, as a sin 11
Matthew, Gospel of, sexuality and 59
Maxiumus the Confessor 65–6
Metropolitan Community Church, gay affirmation and 22
mission, modernity and 126
Moberly, Elizabeth 33
modernity
  anticulture 124–5, 128–9
  applying scripture to 141–5
  changes in sexuality and 7–8
  community, identity and authority 145–9
  conservative and progressive 156–9
  defining terms and xi
  dismantling Trueman's analysis 129–32
  double listening 140–2
  dystopian views of 118–26
  expressive individualism and 123–7
  gulf between worldviews 120–9
  holiness and worldliness 116–18
  interpretation of ix–x
  moral values 132
  as non-Christian 120–3
  non-monstrous 133–7
  phony war over 159–60
  'plastic' sexuality 149–55
  queer theory and 127
  Schaeffer and 120–1
  Stott on evangelical modernity 138–45
  Taylor's multifaceted view 130–1
  Trueman's analysis 123–7
  underlying sexuality debate 115–18
Modernity and Self-Identity (Giddens) 146–9
Moffatt, James 52
Mollenkott, Virginia
  interprets 'against nature' 55
  Is the Homosexual my Neighbor? (with Scanzoni) 28–9
  meaning of *malakoi* 52
moral discourse
  emotivism in 131–2
  guilt-free modernity 150
  MacIntyre and 131–2
  values and community 145, 148
Moss, Roger
  Christians and Homosexuality 27–8

Genesis 19 43
scripture 29
MultiplyX conference 157–8

National Evangelical
  Anglican Conference, Keele
  84–5
Nationwide Festival of Light
  23, 89
Niebuhr, H. Richard, *Christ
  and Culture* 116
Nolland, Lisa, *God, Gays,
  and the Church* (with
  Sugden and Finch, eds)
  107

Oasis Trust 101
O'Donovan, Oliver
  on the debate viii
  doctrinal truth 70–2
  interpreting scripture x
*On the literal interpretation
  of Genesis* (Augustine of
  Hippo) 66

paedophilia
  assumptions about 102
  Schmidt on 94
Paul, Ian
  on Genesis 19 43
  Levitical laws 49
  on liberal scholars 79–80
  on meaning of *qadhesh* 46
Paul the Apostle
  desire 'against nature' 53–7
  encounter on Damascus
    Road 110

vice list 50–7, 69
Peter, Second Letter of
  Testament of Naphtali and
  42
Pittenger, Norman
  *Some notes on an ethics for
  homosexuals* 23
  Time for Consent? 22
The Plausibility Problem
  (Shaw) 110–11
The Post Evangelical
  (Tomlinson) 90
procreation *see* family and
  children
prodigal son(s) 113
progressives
  CEEC and 81–2
  communication or
    apocalypse 109–11
  definitions xi, 158
  evangelical identity against
    84
  extreme positions and
    98–103
  'gay-liberal conspiracy'
    95–6
  issues of interpretation 73–4
  modernity and 118, 156–9
  ordination of women 90
  Paul on wrongness of 79–80
  redrawing the lines 103–5
  theological innovation 1
promiscuity, assumptions
  about 102
Protestantism
  individualism and modernity
    133–6

INDEX OF NAMES AND SUBJECTS

moral law distinctions 48
Purity and Danger (Douglas) 48

qadhesh, meaning of 45–7
queer theory, modernity and 127

Reform opposes LGCM service 92
Rieff, Philip
  anticulture 133
  monstrous modernity 130
  sexuality and culture 152
  Trueman and 123–5
The Returns of Love (Davidson, pseudonym) 24, 111
The Rise and Triumph of the Modern Self (Trueman) 115–16, 123–9
Roberts, Vaughan, vicar of St Ebbe's
  The Beautiful Story video 81
  Paul's vice lists 51, 69
  response to Croft 38
Robertson, Pat 119
Robinson, John, *Honest to God* 22
Roman Catholic Church
  danger in worldliness 118
  Third Lateran Council 41
Romans, First Letter to 31, 52
  Aquinas and 42
  Chrysostom on 64

discussion of homosexuality 39, 41, 53–7, 93
Rome, ancient concepts of sexuality in 6
Runcorn, David, *Love Means Love* 104

Save the Parish movement 157–8
Scanzoni, Letha Dawson
  interprets 'against nature' 55
  Is the Homosexual my neighbor? (with Mollenkott) 28–9
  meaning of *malakoi* 52
scapegoats 87
Schaeffer, Francis
  gospel and modernity 140–1
  on modernity and Christianity 120–1
  'taking the roof off' 120
  Trueman and 123, 125
Schmidt, Thomas E.
  ancient and modern views 56
  Genesis 19 43
  Straight & Narrow 93
  Searching Issues (Gumble) 106
sexual assault, Genesis 19 and 42–4
sexuality
  authenticity and xi
  complementary nature 62–3, 64
  Cornwall and reproduction 136–7

defusing debate 129
early church teaching 63–9
the Fall and 65–6, 71
as first-order issue 82–3, 89, 127–30
fracture lines 112–13
God's intention in creation 30
history of debate vii–x, 78
male-female difference 69–70
misunderstandings in debate viii
modernity and 115–18, 127–9
not complementary 67–9
one-flesh reunion 32, 60–1, 63–9
overwhelming change 1
Paul's vice lists 69
penetrator/penetrated 11, 19
'plastic' 149–55
pre-modern concepts 6–10
procreation as purpose of 9–13, 11
sin outside marriage 2–3
transgender debate 127
see also family and children; homosexuality; marriage, heterosexual; marriage, same-sex
Shaftesbury, Antony Ashley-Cooper, 7th Earl of 14
Shaw, Ed
The Plausibility Problem 110–11
sex and marriage 155
sin
the Fall and sexuality 30, 65–6
homosexuality 2–3
not necessarily criminal 20–1
Situational Ethics (Fletcher) 22
Skinner, Marilyn 6
Slaves, women and homosexuals (Webb) 63
Smith, Christian 123
Society for the Protection of Children (SPCC) 14
Sodom narrative 19, 26–7
'not about sodomy' 43
scriptural scholarship 41–5
sexual assault and 42–4
Some Issues in Human Sexuality (Church of England) 42, 46
Some notes on an ethics for homosexuals (Pittenger) 23
Song of Songs celebration of sexuality 68
Spring Harvest 85
Stott, John 24
on AIDS 103
cites *The Returns of Love* 111
The Contemporary Christian 138–45
differences in interpretation 58
evangelical movement 84, 85

INDEX OF NAMES AND SUBJECTS

fourth edition rewrite 102
on 'gay lifestyle' 94
Gumbel references 106
holiness and worldliness
   116–18
interprets 'against nature'
   55, 56
*Issues Facing Christians
   Today* 6, 17, 31–5, 89, 94
Issues in Human Sexuality 3
Jesus quotes Genesis 59–60
Levitical laws 49
meaning of *malakoi* 52
on meaning of *qadhesh* 46
modernity and
   evangelicalism 138–45
Moss and 28
new interpretations 34
on past homophobia 81
pressure on 101
rejection of homophobia 16
social justice 83–4
Straight & Narrow (Schmidt)
   93
Strangers and Friends (Vasey)
   96
Student Christian Union 84
Sugden, Chris, *God, Gays,
   and the Church* (with
   Nolland and Finch, eds)
   107
syncretism, danger of 125,
   138

Taylor, Charles 125
   community and authority
   145
   expressive individualism
   115
   Giddens and 146
   multifaceted modernity
   130–1, 144
   Reformation and self 133–4
   Trueman and 123
Ten Commandments 51
Testament of Naphtali 42
Thatcher, Margaret 89
Thomas, Santosh 58
Til, Cornelius van 120
Time for Consent? (Pittenger)
   22
Timothy, First Letter to
   discussion of homosexuality
   39
   vice list 50–2
Together in Love and Faith
   (Croft) 104
Tomlinson, Dave, *The Post
   Evangelical* 90
*The Transformation of
   Intimacy* (Giddens) 146–9
Trueman, Carl
   blind spots 143–4
   countercultural sexuality
   149–55
   expressive individualism and
   117, 131, 156
   Giddens and 146
   human dignity 149
   on the Reformation 135
   *The Rise and Triumph of
   the Modern Self* 115–16,
   123–9
   on the sexual revolution xi

Stott and 138–9, 140
tensions in analysis 129–32
Trump, Donald 119
Tyree, Alex, *Walking with Gay Friends* 111

Un/Familiar Theology: Reconceiving Sex, Reproduction and Generativity (Cornwall) 136–7
Unconditional: Rescuing the Gospel from the Gay-vs-Christians Debate (Lee) 103–4
United States, culture wars in 93, 107
Universities and Colleges Christian Fellowship (UCCF) 84, 86

Vasey, Michael
  campaign against 96–7
  evangelical civil war 101
  questions consensus 98
  Strangers and Friends 96–7
Vines, Matthew, *God and the Gay Christian* 104

Walker, Marcus 158
Walking with Gay Friends (Tyree) 111

Wallis, Jim 144
Webb, William J. 49
  Slaves, women and homosexuals 63
Welcoming But Not Affirming (Grenz) 102
Westermarck, Edvard 45
White, John, *Eros Defiled* 27–8, 93; *Eros Redeemed* 93
Williams, Rowan, Archbishop of Canterbury
  evangelical civil war and 99, 101
  plea for moderating language 105–6
  replaces Carey 91
  'wokeness' 134–5
women
  feminism 124
  homosexuality and 13, 19, 54, 56
  ministry of 63, 70
  vote to ordain 89–90
Women and the Church (WATCH) 90
Wright, David, meaning of *arsenokoitai* 52–3

yadha, meaning of 42, 44

www.ingramcontent.com/pod-product-compliance
Lightning Source LLC
Chambersburg PA
CBHW022053290426
44109CB00014B/1088